The Big Trap...

THE BIG TRAP...

Just One Last High

T. Rose

Tiffy Rose LLC
Port St Lucie

ISBN: 978-1-7320331-0-8

LCCN #2018902313

Copyright © 2018 by Tiffy Rose, LLC

All rights reserved

Including the right of reproduction

In whole or in any part in any form

While the public record of events and personal interviews are as accurate as memories and transcription allow

– though condensed and edited –

names and precise locale data have been changed to honor privacy.

DEDICATION

I would like to dedicate this book to my

Best Friend & Mentor

This book would never have come to light if Gideon had not shined so brightly in my Soul.

This man of God, one of the Lord's most dedicated patient, loyal, and loving souls was a true inspiration to me. Gideon pushed me to know myself in deep, meaningful ways and explained God to me in a way that no book was ever able to do for me.

May the Lord continue to bless this disciple as he continues to serve others through HIS word.

Thank you, Gideon,

Always,

Rose

Contents

REVIEWS
ix

ACKNOWLEDGEMENT
x

INTRODUCTION
1

Chapter 1.
CHILDHOOD STOLEN
5

Chapter 2.
FAMILY DID WHAT?
23

Chapter 3.
ANYWHERE BUT HOME
44

Chapter 4.
CLIMBING UP TO FALL HARD
69

Chapter 5.
SHINING BRIGHT!
89

Chapter 6.
IT AIN'T A VICTIMLESS CRIME
110

Chapter 7.
THANK GOD FOR THE EMT'S
133

Chapter 8.
RECOVERY THOUGHTS
143

Chapter 9.
THE LONG ROAD BACK
159

Chapter 10.
CROSSROADS
177

Freedom and Recovery
191

Hotline Information
192

REVIEWS

This is a fantastic book! I recently finished reading it. I was on the edge of my seat for the ending! It not only opened my eyes but helped me to understand what my loved one is going through. How very inspiring to know what can be overcome with God's love. Believe! – Robin Pobst

Thank you, you're an inspiration of survival – Myrna Guerrero

Great Book! It was awesome! – Derrick Williams

What a true inspiration you are to so very many. – James Bowen

Get her book. I couldn't put it down. Relatable in so many ways. We can do this. Loved it. Passing it on Tiffy Rose. So many great words of wisdom and insight. – Peggy White

Just finished a great book by Tiffy Rose. Highly recommend this book for anyone in recovery or struggling with addiction. It's a great read that gives a clear picture of the destruction addiction causes and the hope that can be found in recovery. Thanks for penning this Rose. – Erik Borrell

Tiffy Rose share this everywhere you can please, people need to see and hear about your very inspiring and miraculous journey out of hell.
This book will bring Hope to many lost souls – Liz Moldovan (Author)

ACKNOWLEDGEMENT

Trapped is my story, a true story, but not my story alone.

Beyond family and friends who shared the sights and sounds of growing up in Texas and Florida, there were those whose memories and voices could go beyond my own subjective impressions and recollections and make real the raw substance of my life journey. Willingly, and sometimes unwillingly, family members and childhood friends shared the good they remembered and the bad they wished they did not. The youthful days of fun and laughter, and the uncensored dark and gloomy details of events that could never be forgotten, filled voids and revealed what had remained hidden from their view and my own.

With much fear and apprehension, I returned to neighborhoods and haunts that had been both my playground and my prison, searching for any who might remain from my days chasing the elusive good life in sunny, sandy South Florida.

Some did and a few reluctantly recounted what they witnessed or experienced with insight and enough sordid detail to illuminate the dark and dangerous life they believed I had not survived.

In truth, I owe my life to the caring and compassionate first responders, such as the EMT medics who saved my life more than once, the officers or deputies who arrested me more times than I'd like to remember, the judges, jailers, and guards who accorded me with more respect than I sometimes deserved. They were the good men and women who told me the cold, hard truth about who I was but with higher regard for who I am now.

There are numerous others I owe my recovery to as well, such as the doctors, ministers, nuns, counselors, psychologists, hypnotherapists, and anyone else that crossed my path and tended to my physical and emotional wounds.

All these people, and especially my Lord and Savior, Jesus Christ, eventually guided me to safety and security of self in the imperfect, yet healed soul I am today.

Read my story in the words of those who lived it with me.

INTRODUCTION

This is the last straw.

The pain in my side was excruciating.

The harsh summer sun beating down on my swollen face felt like fire.

Taking slow, shallow breaths of humid, 98-degree air to minimize the pain of my two broken ribs and a swollen gut, felt much like the near-death suffocation I had suffered not so long ago. I could feel the heat of the sandy ground beneath me in the open, vacant lot of the grimy, orange stucco thrift store I had found myself lying in was searing my thinly clothed back and buttocks. My thirst was made worse by the grit that was clinging to my parched lips and stinging in my eyes. I knew I was not safe and could not stay here like this. Kevin's attack last night was sudden, unexpected, and brutal.

I was weak, exposed, and vulnerable in a part of town given over to decay and petty crime by day, and drugs and prostitution by night. I had to find refuge from the debilitating sun and heat before I fell victim to a mugging or rape, or another trip to jail if the police discovered me first.

I willed myself up on hands and knees and slowly began crawling toward the alley where I saw a small array of bushes and scraggly maple trees that I could conceal my body in. The pain in my side, with each reach of my hands as I crawled and dragged myself forward, felt like a knife twisting and cutting my flesh. Every ragged breath forced through my lips brought a low deep moan as I inched slowly across the sand, while the heat coming off the asphalt of the narrow alley scalded my hands and knees. I reached the little, shaded huddle of the chest-high thicket, leaned heavily against a thick tree trunk, and felt a momentary relief to be out of the harsh sun and sight of curious eyes. Peering through the leafy overlapping branches of the bushes, I could see the tiny backyards of the old bungalow houses that lined the residential street I remembered walking down once or twice to score drugs. Maybe I could find the strength to stand up and go search for a water hose to quench my raging thirst; right now, I would gladly trade all the drugs or money in the world for just one drink of water, and maybe a little to splash on my aching face.

A vague memory of the night before began to form slowly in my mind. Kevin's rising anger over my refusal to do a trick's kinky bidding turned into a dark violent rage when I did not produce enough money he needed to feed his own drug habit. I hazily remembered fleeing, bloody and shoeless, from the cheap room I had gone to for the trick. How did this all go so very wrong? Just a few days ago, I was lying in the grass looking up through the wide, green canopy of a tall banyan tree over by the marina, not far from here, daydreaming of another life, of being happy and laughing with my kids. Now, painfully beaten and bruised, I was clawing my way up a different tree fantasizing about cool water touching my tongue and flowing down my parched throat, soothing my churning stomach and dizzy mind while hoping I did not lose consciousness.

The weight of my upper body leaning heavily on the tree produced a sharp reminder of the broken collarbone left unrepaired and neglected from another strung out collision of rebellious willpower and a pimp's rage. I squeezed my eyes shut and held in the scream that might alert someone to my unwanted presence. I tried to breathe slowly and quietly as the little voice inside my head tells me I cannot take any more of this pain. Is it the throbbing physical pain my body is presently enduring or is it this life I have succumbed to? Something has to change.

This drug addict life is just not working anymore. I don't want to die like this, today or any other day. If I don't change, it is going to happen sooner rather than later.

At that moment, I am overcome with a dark, empty feeling as

I think about the years gone by, of who I was before, of what I really am now, and the thoughts deepen my feelings of despair and loneliness.

The world around me began spinning faster and faster as images of what life might have been like flashed and then faded into the darkness.

Silently, I slumped to the ground, hidden in the thicket, drifting away in a kaleidoscope of unconscious childhood memories and all the yesterdays that brought me here today, alone and broken.

1
CHILDHOOD STOLEN

I truly wonder...

At 3 a.m. in the small, dark house in rural Texas, was I, little Tiffany, already so sick of the world that I lived in that I was ready to go far away permanently. What force in the universe pressed in on my gentle soul causing such detachment and isolation at this tender young age? Why would I quietly climb the kitchen counter to get the bottle of little orange baby aspirin? Getting down with this prize, I head to my room to swallow one by one Ma's favorite remedy for all that pained me day or night. Would the whole bottle soothe the ache and end this fear? Did I remember the day my Ma warned me sternly that I could only have one for that toothache or fever? Was screaming, fighting, and drunken voids all I could expect? How was I supposed to react to this loud melee of violence surrounding me day and night?

Was this all that my life was supposed to be? What, if anything, could change it? Was this baby aspirin the best choice I had at avoiding a life that now seems I was destined to endure? Ma was not here now. Pa was far away, too. Who else would stop me from taking one or two, or three and four? There was no one here to stop me. My long, slow, downward spiral had begun at the bottom of an empty bottle of orange baby aspirin. As the light in the room slowly faded to black, I was drawn to an empty and quiet place. A peace I had yearned for as long as I could remember embraced me.

Slowly, in quiet delight, I drifted inward to a place where there was no pain, no tears, no cares, not anything to feel or fear, just dark and still. I was enveloped inside a peaceful place for a soothing and safe existence. I heard small, soft sounds; a murmuring voice, or maybe it was not, I was not really sure. I heard a vaguely familiar sound; it was a safe sound in a place not strange. I was here but not alone, and it was okay. A calming presence letting me know I would be alright. I hear a voice speaking softly, the doctor maybe, as God held me tightly for a moment... and sent me back.

Awaking from the first of many drug-induced deliriums and detours on my life path, I was in a hospital bed under the bright lights of the ER. My stomach was pumped; the overdose protocol was successful. I survived the first overdose and was ready to crawl, climb up, walk, fall down, and be pulled back up again and again. Sheer willful drive and determination to just keep going, even when there seemed little or nothing left to give or hope for, was most of what I could claim as my own identity at this point in my young life and far into the future. Along with a deep but uncertain faith in the existence of a real God of love and hope, I would hold fast to my independence of mind and decisive actions toward any goal or choice once made. Here, under the bright lights of medicine and firm but tender care of doctors and nurses, I was safe and secure for now. Mysteries and uncertainties about my life were emerging from within that would be acknowledged and remembered far in the future and remind me of this day.

What if some part of me was aware of the roads and detours that were ahead for me, the constant fear and loneliness I would feel, the ugliness and despair I would endure before I reached out to that bottle of vodka the first time. What if some part of me already knew there was a choice that I could make, and I had just made it? Was this the first attempt to accept a simple way out or a cry for help? Was I really choosing to die or just get someone, anyone, to notice me and help me? How bad could it have been for me, a small child barely old enough to make seemingly simple choices, to have chosen the permanent escape from a life that had barely begun to unfold?

All I saw was anger, disgust, and hate for the burden I must be. My Pa's cold hostility and impatience revealed his desire not to do anything other than leaving the ER and get back to his drinking. Was this all there was for young me? Was it not for the missed monthly cycle and a noble, chivalrous gesture on his part, would they even be together? I was the unplanned, unexpected offering given to two wayward lovers. Was I a result of just bad timing or a backseat mistake that was accepted? Either way, I was definitely in the way of their desired existence and felt it more each day. Pa, stoically cold and distant, and Ma, a shrill, unrelenting, overbearing woman, made me aware just how burdensome I was, leaving me feeling alone and completely unwanted.

Surely, I could have been scolded for challenging the unknown from innate curiosity, but where was the calm voice, the soothing touch of assurance that should follow the angry admonishment borne of fear to welcome me back from the peril of death? Where was the loving relief that I was still here in their world to live in the dark, little house in Texas? There was none there for me, and the pain of it was leaving its ugly mark on a formative, young mind not sure of purpose or place.

The oft-repeating question in my mind always taunting me was do they really love me? I would ask the same questions again and again. Did they care about me? Was a simple life of being cared about, cared for, reminded I was lovable and loved, wanted and valued, and capable of giving back all I was given and more, even possible?

Could it just be that way? Could I be a part of that happy family? Did they love the shy, little girl playing quietly with teddy bears and dolls? Did they have the desire to share that joy and guide my way in life? Could they live and laugh, hug or be hugged, or show affection to each other or me? Would they come to me when I cried out afraid of the dark and noises outside that woke me late at night and assure me I was not alone to defend myself? Sadly, no. The love I yearned for was replaced with constant fear and uncertainty borne of neglect and isolation. Deprived of security and a sense of well-being instrumental to emotional and physical health, my hopes and dreams of happiness grew dim as I heard the loud voices of Ma and Pa yelling and cursing, "It's your entire fault." Or the rebuttal of, "No, it's your fault and I wish I had never met you." My own inner voice speaks softly, "And I would have never been born to be your burden."

Stolen from me was a healthy, happy childhood that should have been filled with laughter and love, not pain and fear. As days became weeks and weeks became months and months became years, this innocent, hazel-eyed, freckled, brown-haired young girl, who was gentle and quiet, full of hope and curiosity, wanting to love and know love, saw it all drift away. Stolen from me by angry and violent people I called my family; the reality of my childhood was established long before I was born. My parents, as well as my extended family, were caught up in multigenerational addiction of alcoholism, endless conflict, and chaos. Just like tonight, right now.

"Tiff!" my little brother Mikey's frightened voice called out to me. I ran to him and huddled with him on the floor in the corner of the family room near the cold fireplace, bravely trying to comfort him and hold back my own tears. Gently rocking us back and forth with my arms securely embracing Mikey, I told him we would be okay, and that I was going to protect him as the thunder of another fight echoed off the walls.

Like so many other nights, Pa was drunk. The six-foot, three inches, heavily framed, Texas-tanned, beast of a man with steel grey eyes, stood menacingly over Ma shouting a barrage of ugly words threatening to slap her silly to teach her a lesson. Ma, maybe a few inches more than five feet with a lean, sinewy farm girl physique, cowered with arms out, hands opened wide and raised in front of her tear-streaked face defending against a slap or push she knew was coming that would send her sprawling to the floor or hard up against the wall. Her anguished pleas for Pa to please stop, please sit down, please don't hit me, please don't do this anymore, please stop scaring the kids, please, please, would usually end when Ma was sprawled out on the floor wailing loudly or pinned by her shoulders against the wall red-faced and moaning loudly.

On the good nights, if you could call them that, Pa just bellowed and threatened her to make the point he was the man of the house. Ma would stand or sit silent and motionless except for the nodding of her head in agreement to the yes or no that agreed with what he was saying or demanding; always doing her best not to escalate Pa's rage to the physical level she feared if she did not listen intently, not daring to defy him in the nighttime battles. Tonight was one of those times that Pa did not send her to the floor or leave her crumpled against the wall with bright red blood trickling from her lips. Ma held her ground against him, hands up bravely telling him how right he was about so many things, and she would make sure that things changed and changed right then. After many long minutes of pleading, or maybe it was hours, his alcohol-fueled rage calmed for a time, Ma convinced Pa things were going to be done his way tomorrow and cautiously coaxed him to the bedroom.

I took a slow deep breath as the fear and tension holding my body taunt began to fade, and I relaxed the protective hold on my brother hoping there would be no more fighting. My arm hurt where Mikey had squeezed it tightly with both hands clinging to me during the scary ordeal. With a sense of relief, I told Mikey we were okay. I was tired and sleepy, and all I could think of was how much I wanted to go crawl into my bed and pull the covers over my head until it all went away. Ma re-emerged from the bedroom and came to kneel down in front of us, giving us hugs and kisses, telling us in a soothing voice that everything was okay. I closed my eyes hoping it really would be okay and let sleep embrace me in happier times and places.

On those truly good days and nights in our house, free of the verbal or physical brawls, Ma would cook and clean, wash and iron, and sing along with the radio sometimes, usually sipping Kahlua and cream in a tall glass trying to survive the harsh life in the West Texas outback. Pa, when he was home from trucking back and forth across the country and sober, would work around the house and on the homestead doing chores for Ma, or work on his big shiny truck. He had fenced off a big garden plot for Ma one spring, and they had planted corn all the way around the outside with lots of rows of vegetables inside the rows of corn; right in the middle of it all, Pa put a big scarecrow. It was a funny-looking stickman made from tree limbs for arms and legs, some of Pa's old clothes, and one of Ma's funny hats on top of a volleyball head with big red eyebrows of ribbons made from Ma's sewing box. I wasn't scared, but Ma said it scared the birds and buzzards away, and Pa and my uncles would laugh and holler at it when they used it for target practice with their twenty-two rifles. After the smoke cleared from the scarecrow shootouts, we would pick the undamaged corn, beans, tomatoes, and other stuff that was growing, to cook for the Sunday summer picnics. There was another dimension of our family and the clan of relatives that made good days too few.

I was born into a largely dysfunctional family. This expanded family of generational differences and cultural bias with limited education fueled their near-endless alcohol-heated debates on every subject. War and racism were favored topics among the alpha male supremacists. Vying for ideological victory in the shadow of Vietnam, race riots coast to coast, and the perils of pot-smoking, hippie homosexuals taking over the world, they ranted and bellowed with fervor when an opportunity presented itself. Macho male angst had trapped them at birth in a cycle of winner take all or guilty ambivalence to be the breadwinners and caretakers of their women and brood. The sly women among them wisely indulged this attitude, getting what they wanted along the way, and letting their man beat his chest for the privilege of their work in the kitchen and company in the bedroom. The balance of female counterparts, like-minded, gossipy types with low self-esteem and helpless dispositions, always vying for social recognition and acceptance, were contentious drama queens. Whether touting the joy of birth control pills in the time of free love or the evil of pornography that men liked, they would cuss, scream, pull hair, and fight with a little provocation on many occasions that brought them together.

Was feuding and fighting the true purpose of the regular gatherings at our house? Where aunts and uncles, and all the others; in-laws, friends, big broods of children, and new strangers met at the favorite bar in town, who were invited along just to be an audience? Not just at our place, but just about anywhere they could gather, was the right place to join in on another drunken brawl. Most of the kids of my kinfolk, including myself, heard and saw the repeating spectacle often enough that it was, to us, an integral part of family culture expressed as, "Being Family." It wasn't just the influence of the family gatherings that exposed the deep-seated and long-held prejudice with simmering resentments. Anger at all things authoritarian and general dissatisfaction with their social status was often the focus of many conversations. This environment created a toxic atmosphere for young children whose minds were being filled with hatred. Unfortunately, there were not enough positive words and acts of kindness to counteract the negative influences for my younger kin and me. Maybe more damning was the increasingly unhappy reality and open hostilities at home that was truly the destructive norm. Ma and Pa were always at war over something. With a few drinks and a few differences of opinion, Ma and Pa easily advanced from screaming and name-calling to throwing punches making sure their victory was secure and their position unchallengeable forever. Any time was a good time, it seemed, to toss a few back and revisit the same differences and fight the same battles again. I surely did not see or understand why "and have a good time," usually meant advancing levels of brutality.

I surely did not see or understand why, and have a 'good time,' usually meant things would fly thru the air intent on hurting each other or whoever else got in the way. Quite often, that meant my little brother Mikey and I. Did they not see the damage that was happening, not only to my brother and me but to our cousins who also lived within the same dysfunctional parameters?

There was a very small, but important, alternate reality illuminated during the early years that was significant. On those nights when Ma and Pa occasionally left me and Mikey at Aunt Hazel's warm, little cottage down by the railroad tracks while they would go visit old friends in East Texas a few times a year, I heard with a hopeful heart about lots of happy children in big, happy families; Aunt Hazel made me smile and laugh until I fell asleep thinking I was in the stories, too. It was only then that I would feel a glimmer of hope for the future. Those happy families and life models in Aunt Hazel's books were the way I had hoped my life could be someday. Those happy, fun-filled lives they lived were not what I was living. My life was a harsh existence filled with grown-up realities of near-constant strife and struggle. I liked snuggling up to Aunt Hazel as she read to me and we would watch and laugh as Auntie's kittens played together, tackling one another and chasing after the ball of yarn she had given them. My favorite was the little one that I named Mittens; he was a lovable black and white striped tabby cat with pure white paws. He would come up to me and rub his body against my legs as he meowed for a drink of milk or requesting a scratch on his head. Mittens always made me smile whenever I got to play with him and his little sister. Jazzy was timid, perhaps she too had been hurt, and fear made her that way. The mommy cat Tigger was a big, slow-walking picture of happy and well-fed. She would just lay out in the yard, occasionally gazing over to me to protectively check on her kittens. I would learn quickly that my childhood would not be anything like the ones in the books Aunt Hazel read to me.

On one particular summer day when all seemed well and we were all trying to stay out of Pa's way because he was already half-drunk, the unexpected happened. The gloom and dark of a summer storm outside had left Mikey and me without alternatives except to stay inside and find something to engage our minds and our boundless energy. A quiet game of hide-and-seek was proceeding well for Mikey and me when something suddenly falls. Mikey had bumped a table and the lamp that was sitting on it toppled to the floor. When the sound of breaking glass filled the room, we froze and stared at one another in disbelief; with fear consuming us, we hoped we could escape what surely was coming. Pa stormed into the room and screamed, "What the hell did you do?" Neither of us could speak, fear paralyzing us as Pa's dark glare pierced our hearts. Little Mikey looked at me and then back at Pa with wide-eyed fear and began to tremble. I had seen that look before and knowing my little brother was about to be beaten, I overcame my own fear and moved in close to protect him. Wrapping my arms around him tightly, I pulled him behind me to shield him from the blows he was going to receive. I screamed, "Please Pa, don't!"

"Stop, you're hurting us!" I took multiple clinched-fist punches to the body before toppling to the floor, all the while holding tightly to Mikey. Finally, the angry giant's rage ceased, and he staggered from the living room leaving us clinging to one another, dazed and crying. Mikey was spared, and the look of sorrow and despair in his eyes burned in me knowing it would not be the last time we would endure the needless drunken cruelty. For the moment, Mikey was safe, and that was all I cared about; a look of relief appeared and replaced the tears on Mikey's face as I stood up and pulled him up close with a reassuring hug and whispering words of forgiveness, "It wasn't your fault; it'll be okay Mikey. We are okay now." Slowly, his trembling subsided, and a look of relief appeared on his face knowing I understood and did not blame him for our ugly misfortune.

I understood somewhere in my mind that I had to be strong for both of us if we were to survive the maniacal tyranny and rage of a brute father that would come again and again. The survival conditioning had formed defensive thinking to avoid the constant looming menace of emotional and physical abuse of everyday life both of us would endure. Quiet desperation was raising barriers to seeking affection and approval. I felt the only safe course was to not make a noise, don't ask for anything, and surely never contradict the accusations or belittlement that assailed us, or it will only be worse, or maybe fatal, for both of us.

As if on cue, when the noise had safely subsided Ma appeared and yelled, "Go to your rooms, now!" Off we ran as fast as possible. I sat quietly shaking in my room listening to Ma complain as she cleaned up the broken lamp. I was defying tears to come, curled up with my tattered raggedy brown teddy bear that had become my best friend long, long ago when life was almost okay. Feeling the heat in my arms and legs rise as the bruises began to form, the emotional pain felt far worse than the sore black and blue muscles. I finally let go and fell asleep asking God to help us. Later that evening during dinner, I was nervously picking at my meatloaf thinking about how much my back hurt when from behind me Ma barked, "What the hell are you doing?" I jumped halfway out of my skin expecting to be slapped again. "Don't play with your food," Ma ordered and stomped out of the kitchen. Such was a day and night in my and Mikey's austere life. We were only preadolescent children and not yet capable of knowing and understanding how and why we would emerge from our journey hardened and disillusioned adults.

On that first day of school when I was in the first grade, I tried to hide the dark, black and blue bruises on my legs and my shame with an ankle-length dress. I struggled emotionally with whom I might let into my private world. Whom do you dare let know the secrets of home, the loneliness, and despair? How would others react? Do I reach out to others to share myself and share in their worlds? Can I really make friends or not? Should I even try? I sensed somewhere that doing so would create even more disappointments, so why bother? Why take the chance?

I had feared that first day at school for some time, and as it grew closer so, too, did the uneasy feeling in my belly, as well as increased the stress of ridicule or shame of things I hid inside. And then sadly, brutality came again only a day before and with it an overpowering fear of going at all. Who would or could protect me except God and myself? I knew that there was a loving protective God somewhere out there or in me somewhere because I could always remember hearing that small, calming voice in the ER after taking all those little orange pills. It had to be God because Aunt Hazel had talked about Him and told me He loved me. It must have been His voice, I had secretly told Aunt Hazel, that was speaking to me.

I was embarrassed by who I was and the home I came from. Who would want to know about me and all those things going on in my world? I could not and would not let anyone know; I shut down inside and raised barriers to protect myself. Just be quiet, keep your distance, and do not let anyone too close, I told myself. Quiet and demure, obedient to a fault, a hard, straight-ahead stare focused on my teacher's every word; I held tight to a refuge of self-control. I was exposed, and there was no place to hide at school except in devotion to my teacher's instructions and the work I was given to do. Among so many kids laughing, giggling, making funny faces, and sometimes peeing in their pants, the relief from the fear-inducing noise at home was calming while I was there. I spoke only when my teacher called on me and generally ignored and avoided the other kids' attempts to engage me. At most, a solemn yes, no, I don't know, or I can't do that, was the extent of conversation I had with my classmates. After a time, they stopped the quest for my attention. The choice of emotional solitude at school, once made, would be fatefully unfortunate for me. The behavior and good grades I achieved were consistently praised by my teachers, but over time produced overt disdain from many of my less disciplined classmates who resentfully labeled me a teacher's pet. At home, the consistent "A" on my report cards for Behavior and Academic Achievement went all but virtually unnoticed, receiving a cursory 'good work' or 'great job' only a handful of times. Paradoxically, the self-imposed discipline and dedication yielded little emotional acknowledgment from those I needed it from most. Sadly, forty years would pass by before the harsh, self-imposed exile could be permeated, and I would allow myself to be loved and accepted by others. Or would I really hear God's voice speaking to me?

How is a normal, loving, healthy childhood filled with happy curiosity and laughter different from the childhood my brother and I experienced? I didn't get the smiles and supportive encouragement when those first shaky steps were taken, when the potty was mastered, when the colorful scribbles appeared as an alphabet when the first tricycle was ridden, or a host of other giant leaps. Also, absent was the encouragement for initiative and independence when adventuring across the big unknown space called the backyard, the kisses on the head when bumping the coffee table, or skinned knee from falling off the bike. Missing, too, were the hugs and smiles when the first "A" on the report card came, or the celebratory "Happy Birthday" party year after year. The formulas for creating happy children, emotionally stable teenagers, and successful adults can be found in instructional magazines, countless how-to books, and even older generations. Sadly, no one in my childhood other than Aunt Hazel read even one of those books. I don't know any adults in my extended family who, consequently, have more than two dozen kids between them read a single book on how to be a successful parent. Maybe that was why almost half of all my cousins went to jail at least once and two of them for most of their life.

LOVE! More importantly, unconditional love, is what all children born into this world deserve.

Unfortunately, innate, moral obligations to nurture children from birth to adulthood of the next generation, seem to be lacking in our society more and more frequently. I believe that a majority of the "okay" children who are raised in the ideal, two-parent home have a normal, happy childhood and grow to become productive, upstanding citizens in our society. However, what about all the others who do not have the same equal chance? A child not planned or ever wanted? Children raised by single parents, aunts and uncles, grandparents? What do their stories sound like? How many follow a doomed path, and how many escape and never share their story with anyone? Why do so many of us try to fix ourselves and our problems with alcohol and drugs?

What must childhood be like for a baby created by ill-informed high school teenagers in the back seat of a car, or the child of countless peer-pressured unwed mothers who drop out of school to go it alone when the boyfriends yell whore and slut and run away to avoid responsibility? More than likely, the innocent new baby or child is left to cope with their difficult future without much support. How many little voices whose happy sounds are replaced and dispossessed by cries of fear, and moans of anguish, as their lives unfold in a world of hard loveless realities and hope unfulfilled? Not uncommon today, a generational trend continues stronger than ever wherein stable, loving grandparents, willing or unwilling, are haplessly given the task of raising their grandchildren due to their own, once-perfect child untimely discovery of drugs, alcohol, or both and withdrawing from the responsibility of parenting.

Not alone do grandparents inherit anew the child-rearing role, but they are most often the first choice followed closely by sisters and aunts, whose natural maternal instincts and abilities, make them primary beneficiaries of the steadily, increasing population, of neglected or unwanted children displaced by alcohol and drugs.

When any child is fortunate enough to grow up in a two-parent household, they usually fare much better than children raised in the alternative of the single-parent homes, by relatives, or the array of foster care programs that steadily increase in numbers daily. It would be unfair to say the children raised in a two-parent household always have it easier or better, but the disparities between the two environments are significant and easily observable. I guess I was fortunate because I had two parents, though they never really appeared to want each other, or to be parents, much less seem to enjoy each other or us. So, where was I supposed to learn or understand what love is or the repercussions of what the lack of it could mean? Not until late in life, after many things had gone terribly wrong, did I learn that the lack of affectionate love and lack of any real, nurturing in childhood would have terrible consequences.

All too often, it is a single-parent household where a lack of necessary resources creates daunting and insurmountable challenges to healthy growth. Often unstable and unpredictable in terms of safety, security, food on the table, and educational support – all the basic ingredients for a child to grow and prosper to his or her full potential are simply not there. However, these single parents usually try hard and some even succeed. A child born bereft of growth and a developmental roadmap can cause them to be helpless and dependent on a caregiver who is, more often than not, at the same disadvantage; therefore this child does not often reach his or her full potential. This shared plight often results in emotionally empty or adverse relationships without sufficient positive attributes for success for either the parent or the child.

The family environment in my own and many other addicts' childhood share the same negative factors as one finds in single-parent households, for instance abusive, unstable, emotionally unpredictable, barren of many joyful or happy events, as well as the terrible effects of substance abuse. Not to mention, limited educational achievement, limited employment or work stability for the parent, parents, or caregivers, a child or children add more emotional and financial hardships. Just as my little brother and I did and very early, we knew we did.

<u>Again, why do so many of us try to fix ourselves with alcohol and drugs?</u>

Growing in this unhealthy life garden are other negative factors that can lead to various forms of addiction, such as when children are regularly stuck in front of the TV for unlimited amounts of time or dismissively sent to their rooms to play alone and be out of the way; these can often produce negative emotional dispositions. Parents that are unable to join in their lives or who don't actively participate in the emotional growth process of their children, leave a huge empty chasm where normal healthy life-shaping interactions could and should have been.

How many children today continue to grow up in emotional isolation? How many are surrounded by increasing amounts of TV and real-life violence in their own neighborhoods? How many kids today will suffer the same fate as me, my brother, and most of my cousins did a generation ago? Largelyleft to raise ourselves in a harsh, hostile, violent, and unforgiving environment, we had too many opportunities with limited guidance to make bad decisions and wrong choices, and we did. Many of them would repeat over, and over again. How many of us, in how many generations, will watch as our parents abuse themselves and each other, and in turn abandon or abuse their own children and continue the vicious dysfunctional cycle? I only hope and pray that you and I are among the last.

Let me share with you a few more of the unfortunate dilemmas that ultimately guided my own steady journey into addiction. Like most people, I had goals for my life and a plan of action on how to obtain them and how I would become that person. I thought I prepared myself for the consequences and outcomes of my decisions, but I would later learn that I absolutely did not know or understand how my actions had unexpected consequences. What my choices affected or controlled. I most always thought at those critical junctures that I did know, but I was too young and inexperienced as a teenager, and later as an adult in denial, to accept I absolutely did not and because I did not, bad situations often progressed to worse, and any choice I had at that point could not be good. The decisions I made were determined by which choices would be the least painful or which would enable me to remain blissfully high the longest to avoid unresolved emotional conflict and its pain.

Ultimately, I became so naively self-assured by the very effects of the drugs themselves that the happiness I spent so much of my life searching for could only be maintained through drug use. This is, perhaps, the most treacherous and troublesome but real dilemma nearly every addict has or will face managing physical or emotional pain, or both. In a time when most all medication prescribed for pain has psychoactive attributes that are not universal in everyone using them, nor one hundred percent predictable in the complete range of side effects that can occur, anyone taking them is susceptible to potential abuse or addiction. Most all of the effective pain medications prescribed in varying dosages for both physical and physiological relief pose a risk for addiction when taken for either category if not taken exactly as prescribed for the time the doctor has set for the patient.

For many of us, drugs, especially highly addictive drugs, were at least a partial solution to organic or psychological illnesses experienced at one or multiple points in our lives. Whether determined by self-directed choice or medically diagnosed, the substance chosen or prescribed lessened or relieved pain in one or more of its many forms. The experience of physical pain or emotional discomfort at whatever level is something most normal people seek to avoid, or at least diminish, and because that is true, drug use, substance abuse, addiction, and any other label applied, will continue to be problematic for us as individuals and create ever-larger medical and social conflicts of which you and I are apart. I was hooked on illegal drugs when a couple of hits on a marijuana joint relieved, for a few moments, the ever-present emotional pain of childhood traumas; and a dysfunctional alcohol-abusing family growing steadily within me. It progressed from there. Eliminating any or all of the following issues might have deterred the first, self-directed escape from my unfortunate reality and multiple near-death overdoses; a more stable family life, not being physically abused, access to medical care when it was needed, and not being raped by a family member. Ultimately, it would be the medics who saved my life, as well as all of the individuals who reached out to help me find my own truth that helped me overcome addiction and, at least partially, resolve the underlying causes.

This story, my journey into the darkness of drug addiction and the hard road out to sobriety and freedom, is true.

It's gritty and unsanitized because less so would be a dishonest deception and a distortion of the truth that I and others experienced. Maybe it is your story, too. With a few names and places changed, you and I have known the same pains and pleasures, the same tears and laughter, the same hopes and dreams shattered and reborn anew, clean and sober. Therefore, my own honest reality is necessary.

If you are still on your journey to freedom, maybe you will discover through my story you are not alone, there is a real way out, and your dreams are not as unattainable as you might think they are right now. Above all, you or that someone you know did not get addicted because they wanted to nor did they do it alone. Someone or many someones helped each of us to become trapped. It will be the same to escape to freedom and safe from relapse, we all need someone. After the hard personal choice is made to be addiction-free, reach out for a hand to help you on the journey because you can't go it alone.

2

FAMILY DID WHAT?

During my grade school years, I endured increasing amounts of physical violence. My drunken Pa would use me as a punching bag. A small thing, a big thing, or nothing at all I was an easy outlet for his physical and violent aggression and so rarely his affection. Whenever my mother was out doing whatever she could to help support the family, his violence would find its way to me fast and hard. His rage, when fueled by alcohol of copious amounts, became physical when cursing and shouting obscenities was not sufficient to satisfy his mercurial dominance over Ma, Mikey, or me. Without warning and with the smallest of unintentional provocation, Pa's fist, feet, belt, or the closest object nearby would deliver his lethal intent. No amount of crying, pleading, or begging would subdue his compulsion and urgency to inflict pain as punishment. Even without the alcohol, he was an angry man, defiant of any authority, and demanded varying degrees of submission from all around him.

Ma was a reliable and regular victim for Pa's rage and physical violence. For failing to adequately meet his needs as he stated so often, she was no good for nothin' and deserved whatever hurt he would inflict on her. Very rarely what she did was adequate for him, and it was always her fault. It was his right as the man of the house, he proclaimed, for puttin' a roof over our heads, food in our bellies, and clothes on our backs to punish her so she would learn to do right by him. I overheard her coldly admit to my aunt many years later that she would stay away from home as often as possible to avoid his rage and abuse which, consequently, allowed her to turn a blind eye to the abuse my little brother and I would experience in her place. I never forgot what I heard.

Pa would occasionally go to great lengths to justify the abuse he doled out. His pleading defense when he was sober and remorseful was "He loved us all, and we didn't know how hard he had to work to make us all happy." On and on he would wail in his defense. In his mind, he was protecting us from the real world, so we should be grateful and love him back. Always his repeated description of what love and loving was or wasn't made him innocent of being the monster he truly was. His anger issues, his drinking, and his dislike of being told what to do inflicted heavy burdens of another kind upon us all. I remember the many times he successfully reduced us to near financial poverty of lengthy duration. Far worse, he produced emotional poverty that would leave permanent scars inside and out on Ma, Mikey, and myself.

Love? I guess that is what I thought it was sometimes. I grew up believing anxiety, fear, humiliation, shame, pain, and guilt are what you felt when someone "loved" you. Surely, Ma felt the same emotional pain and void of love as I did. Could it be that she, too, was an innocent child victim and knew no better? If she were, would she admit to it? Does she stay, as so many women do, afraid to admit it and live clinging to a fantasy myth of a happy marriage for purposes of self-protection and social acceptance? I still don't know today.

Ma worked all the time, finding some measure of safety there and staying away from the abusive tyranny at home. Therefore, much of Ma's family responsibilities became mine, and they started at sunrise. Each morning Ma would come in to wake me and remind me of the daily tasks that I already knew by heart. Instructions, more akin to orders, were to pack school lunches for Mikey and me, prepare breakfast for both of us, before I woke him, help him get dressed, if needed, and lastly make sure everything was cleaned up and put away before getting us both out the door on time to catch the bus for school. With lunches and books in hand, rain or shine, and sometimes snow, we walked a half-mile up a low hill to wait for the old yellow school bus. I actually enjoyed the peaceful quiet of the morning pulling Mikey along. I felt the big sister, and motherly role, while Mikey always showed his appreciation for the way I treated him and listened to what was on his mind during our daily sojourns to and from the bus stop. I took pride in that I was a big girl, and my independence of mind and action was guiding us both. It was the calm and peace that I needed for the day ahead.

I didn't have any friends, but on one particular day, I met Amber. The day was quite like any other late fall day, with birds singing in the cool, morning air, and the bright sun barely rising by the time we reached our bus stop. While climbing aboard the bus and looking for a seat, I spotted a girl who would become my new friend. Her name was Amber, and she slid over letting me sit down as Mikey found a seat in front of me. Due to Amber's persistent efforts, I had slowly, with great caution and apprehension, lowered my survival defenses against letting anyone get close and seeing the ugly of my life at home. Amber, also lived in a very harsh emotional environment at home, but we overcome our mutual fears of others and became friends. We talked about the new boy up front who just moved into the house down the hill and we would giggle about how cute he looked. We would talk about the homework assignment we had to complete the night before, wondering if it was correct. Neither of us had anyone to help us with our homework other than demanding parents with little interest in our academics, other than insisting it is completed before going to bed.

I loved school. Math was one of my favorite subjects, and I liked Ms. Carter, my teacher. I looked forward to playing with my friends at school now, after spending a lot of time solemn and on defensive self-imposed isolation from any interaction. Amber and a few carefully chosen others were the only things that kept me from completely shutting down emotionally again. Running around the playground at recess laughing and swinging on new gym equipment the school had just put up, I was glad to be away from home. Safe at school to quietly spend my scarce and precious free time daydreaming just a little of what life might be like without the constant stress at home, school was the only place of refuge for my mind and body.

Sadly, the school day for me was too short. When it was time to board the bus for home, my heart would sink as that uneasy feeling in my stomach would rise and burn as the bus stop grew closer. The two of us would begin our walk home as we talked about the day. I let the array of things that must be done before bed arrange themselves in my mind. Ma always made lists to follow for each day of the week, and my routine for a school day was thumb-tacked to the wall near the refrigerator.

Homework was not usually at the top of the list, but I usually did it first because the A's on my report card was a source of approval from my teachers that I desperately needed in order to survive. The house and the porches were to be swept and vacuumed, the dishes cleaned and put away, and any clothes Ma had washed and put on the line that day were to be taken down and put in the basket. I dutifully did as told without fail every day. Lucky for me, I was still too young to wash clothes or cook dinner in addition to the rest of my chores, but I would usually volunteer and regularly do it anyway hoping to get a token of approval for my effort, but rarely did that happen. After making sure Mikey got his homework completed and all my chores were done, I would sometimes let myself daydream a little with only a small amount of ever-present fear of something simmering just beneath the surface. Sometimes simple whimsical thoughts of places and happy events in Aunt Hazel's stories would give me a reason to believe the future could be anything I could imagine. I could be in a faraway place where people were warm and friendly and there were many fun things to do. I could imagine myself as a princess with a prince by my side, riding horses and going to a ball dressed up in a pretty gown wearing a crown, and dancing with my prince. Maybe I could be a ballerina one day too and have flowers thrown at my feet. Maybe my dreams of going to live by the ocean could happen, and I hoped it would. My daydreams were just about being wanted and loved and being someplace that was safe from the hostilities and turmoil that were present in my life.

The real-life I was living was harsh and emotionally demanding. There were not enough slow and simple kind of days without stress and worry to experience. A calendar holiday, an anniversary, some birthdays, or most of the big family party's didn't induce the expected cheerfulness but added to the tumult and unease in my life. Everyone possible was invited; family, friends, and acquaintances that were nearer stranger than not. Alcohol, too often in excess, made the gatherings rowdy and raucous, and contentious but in a friendly way. Adults getting drunk, parents half watching their kids or screaming at them when they were unruly, and everyone yelling about whatever crossed their intoxicated minds. However, in the loud cacophony of celebration, the sound of loneliness echoed in my soul.

Ma would dress me up in little frilly dresses she so proudly found at the Salvation Army stores in town. When the other mothers showed up, she bragged to them about the time and effort she put into making her little precious girl acceptable to the world, and so she could measure up how much better I was dressed. Oh, how I hated it. Like a toddler put on display for the world to admire, the shy and still innocent young girl felt obliged to smile and be noticed, not for herself but Ma's unabashed need for approval wherever and whenever she could muster it. I was told to stay close to the house and stay clean because Ma didn't want me in the stinky barn all dressed up in my party dress and shoes.

I really didn't want to be paraded around, as I could not stand those uncomfortable dresses and ill-fitting shoes, but I never let it show. I liked my clothes plain and simple, and I liked wearing shoes that were tough and durable; they felt better on my feet. I kept them clean and wore them until my feet would not go in them anymore. It was during one of these family gatherings when my cousins Monica, Tina, Susie, and I were running around the yard laughing and having fun as eight-year-olds do when evil came calling up close and personal.

I was indeed a girl, but the big, old oak tree in the yard did not stop me from being something of a tomboy on occasion. More than once, I had climbed almost to the top of the tree when our parents were not watching. Today was no different. On a dare from my cousins, I climbed up the tree wearing this yucky yellow dress. The girls were all laughing at me as I did, saying they could see my underwear showing beneath the dress. I knelt on a branch, tucked the dress up close around my knee line, and worked my way unsteadily down the tree, embarrassed by the taunt. I was climbing down from the tree as my cousins ran off to answer the call of their parents. I was thinking I was alone when I heard a voice calling out to me. My cousin, Pete, came walking up from behind the house, he took me by the hand, and said, "Come on Tiffy, I want to show you something in the barn."

Wow! I had always been very curious about what the older kids were doing out there in the barn; maybe now I would finally find out. As the loud and rowdy party carried on with the sound of bottles clanking and the smell of ribs in the smoker filling the air, no one noticed, or maybe did not care, when I disappeared from sight. Pete knew nobody was paying attention, and he had made certain of it, and I would soon discover why.

I had never played with any other kids outside of family and these events, especially boys, except at school during recess. I was so excited to be able to play with the older kids, and Pete had always been nice to me on the few occasions his family had come out here in the country to visit. I went skipping alongside Pete curious to see what the allure the barn held for the big kids. At eight years old, the world was still full of simple excitement and new discoveries. The barn was someplace I could go only when accompanied by my parents or the big kids who on the few occasions when they came, would work baling hay or milk the neighbor's cow. Today, the discovery would not be one that I would ever forget. When we reached the big, red barn, Pete pulled open the heavy wooden door for us to go through, and the strong smell of the big stacks of baled hay billowed out and made me sneeze. At the door, I sneezed once, twice, and three times. I was walking and listening to Pete as he pointed ahead saying, "Down there just past the last stalls – down there, that's where they are hiding." Walking slowly along, peering into each of the empty stalls that we passed, I looked for the other kids I had expected to be here. I am puzzled and ask Pete, "Where are Monica and Tina? Aren't they in here? Are they hiding from us? Is Susie hiding, too?" I was eagerly anticipating seeing something cool to answer my questions of what was going on in this mysterious place I was forbidden to go.

I sense something is wrong and realized no one else was really waiting in the barn. Because I was curious to know what the older kids did out here, that has kept me from this secret world until now, I continued. When we get near the last stall, I spotted the friendly old mare Honey, drinking from her water bucket. The big, brown eyes of Honey gaze briefly at me as if wanting to say, "Run, Tiff, run!" But she goes back to her water bucket for another drink and pays no more attention to our presence. My cousins that I had seen come this way earlier in the day definitely were not here now. Maybe they had gone off to the swimming hole, just beyond the tree line that was the boundary of my world, to have their own secret drinking fest with the liquor they had swiped away from the party.

Suddenly, Pete stopped walking, grabbed me, and forcefully coaxed me along into a corner of the last semi-dark stall and started rubbing on my body. I was dumbfounded and didn't understand what is happening. I went rigid and felt a knot of fear in my stomach. Fear, like the time I lost the two quarters for my and Mikey's school lunch and knew I would be whipped or beaten by Pa that night. This is not going to be okay, I sensed, knowing I needed to get away from Pete. I see Pete unzip his pants, put his hand inside his pants, and hear him grunt a small funny sound. When he took his hand out of his pants, he is holding his penis. Ma called it a 'penis' when I had asked why Mikey's privates were different from mine down there while we were being bathed naked under the garden hose in the yard one day. Pete started rubbing his penis, and I was confused because I thought that we were going to play some big-kid game out here. I didn't understand what was happening or why Pete was doing what he was doing with me here.

Pete swiftly reached under my dress and began to rub my bare chest. The uneasy sensation in my stomach increased, and my throat tightened as my confusion turned into rising panic. His cold, rough hand forcefully rubbing and squeezing my soft skin was painful, and I wanted Pete to stop hurting me. Before I could say 'stop,' Pete quickly slid his hand down inside my panties, and I froze as a new kind of terror grabbed me while Pete started rubbing on my girl parts. I was suddenly unsure if I should yell for help or let him continue as a strange and unknown feeling happened. A tingling sensation, a kind of good thing I had never felt before began to run thru me. That natural, female response, that happens even if you really don't want it to, was happening to me.

I hardly even heard Pete say, "Do you like that?"

Or, a few long moments later his demanding voice saying, "Here – Lick it!"

Dazed and vaguely curious of the new sensations but knowing I shouldn't be out here doing anything like this made the vague conflict I was experiencing grow more ominous. I remembered how the Minister down at the church preached about being good, and I knew being in a big, dark barn that I was forbidden from entering alone, was definitely not 'being good' right now. My youthful hesitancy to act on my emotional dilemma, ended abruptly when Pete's loud voice snapped me back to where I was and how I got there as he yelled at me again, "Lick it, Girl!" Horror struck me like a punch in the gut from my daddy. With one hand, still rubbing on my bald little private parts Pete grabbed at my head with his other and forcefully pushed it down towards his penis. This evil had a hold of me and an innocent child was forcefully exposed to worldly flesh desires without my consent. "Lick it, girl," Pete screamed again.

The Evil, demanding tone in his voice frightened me even more than knowing daddy was going to beat me if he found out I was in the barn with Pete. A voice in my head shouted, "Run Tiff! Run now!" Horrified, I pushed Pete away, screamed at the top of my lungs, and bolted for the house running faster than ever before while he was shouting at me from the barn. When I reached the safety of the front porch without Ma and Pa seeing me, I stopped and looked back hoping and praying Pete was not right behind me. I realized I had scared him. I had shown him I was not going to let him force me to do those things I did not want to do. Maybe his other victims had let him do those things, but I was not going to, not ever. I knew, now, that I could fight back, and it spooked him that I did not allow him to dominate me.

His voice rang in my ears all the way back to the house as he yelled, "Don't you go telling anyone, Tiff, or I'll make you pay." I had just experienced Rape.

Forced to do any sexual act, at any age, at any time, is always Rape. No is No. Discovering my sexuality and having intimate relations with the opposite sex, should have remained for pleasing discovery many years ahead. Now I was left to figure out, on my own, just what happened and why. What was this tingling feeling of adrenaline running thru me, a lingering feeling of something mysterious, exciting, and secret I had never experienced? Why did I feel something right was in there, somewhere, but feel it was so wrong at the same time? I felt scared and betrayed by my older cousin. He had done something very wrong, and he knew it.

A family is supposed to protect one another, not this wrong whatever it was kind of thing, Pete had just done to me. What he didn't know was that it would haunt me for the rest of my life. A rising sense of alarm sent me running back to the party to find my younger cousins and warn them. I had to tell them about what happened to me in the barn with Pete. I find Monica and my other two cousins playing at the big tire swing. "There you are, Tiffy. We have been looking for you. What did Cousin Pete show you out in the barn? We heard him call you; did you see something cool out there in the barn? I wish I could go out there too," Monica said gleefully. "Listen stay out of that stinky barn, and Pete is a jerk. Don't play with him," I warned.

"OK we won't Tiffy," they all answered in agreement before running off to play. I immediately wondered if I should have been harsher with my warning to them. Should I have told them anything else? It would have to be enough for now, and I would be observant so that nothing happened to them today. 'Thank you God for protecting me,' said the small voice in my head.

The sounds of loud music and a cacophony of party voices brought me out of the lingering daze of confusion and concern I felt for my cousins and I. Startled by the sound of Pete's voice a few feet behind me, I turned around to find him standing right there. "Better not tell Tiffany, you better not tell anyone," he said with a glaring look of defiance. A jolt ran through me, and the hairs on the back of my neck stood up. I couldn't or wouldn't speak and after a long moment, Pete turned and slowly walked away leaving me certain I had just seen something dark and evil. Pete was not at all who I had thought he was. I understood instinctively, now, what I was sensing when Pete would sulk around looking at my girl cousins and me. It was about what had just happened to me; it was about those things that we were not supposed to do, those things that were not supposed to happen with family. I knew I had barely escaped from something far worse and uglier than the fondling I had endured. I never said a word to anyone, and really, seriously, who am I going to tell? The ugly truth was no one cared enough to listen. Pa would have probably beaten me for telling such lies about cousin Pete, and well, there's Ma who would agree with Pa. Neither of them was much interested in my welfare either, so I simply kept silent.

Between school and home, I was always busy. My schoolwork was important to me and was a source of pride and achievement, so I gave it my best efforts every day. The chores at home were always there to do, and I did them without complaining, but also without receiving much appreciation for doing them. Even when I was sick a few times with the flu or the measles, I still tried to do my chores. If I didn't, Ma would say I was just being lazy and didn't care about how hard she herself had to work. When Mikey got the measles a few days after me, Ma said it was my fault because I had been playing in the dirt in the garden, and that's what made Mikey and I get sick. I was given more and more responsibility for Mikey because Ma was not home as much after a new friend had moved into a little house a few miles away. Ms. Libby, as Ma called her, did not have any kids. She also worked at the grocery store in town, so Ms. Libby and Ma spent a lot of their time after work doing stuff, and when Pa was on the road trucking, Ma did not come home until dark.

Pa was gone a lot after he took a new job, with a big cross-country trucking company. Sometimes, he would be gone for just a week and be home for a few days and then take off again. The big weekend drunk parties that were so much a regular part of life were less frequent, and there wasn't as much fighting at home either. The fights became more infrequent when Pa's job required him to be gone for a month or more at a time. Also, he was often not home when family and friends would come to the Baker place for a party. The garden, with the corn and all the vegetables, wasn't torn up so bad either. I learned how to help Ma jar a lot of food that had grown in the garden; we had enough to fill all the cupboards and still be able to give some away. The downside to Pa being gone was that he missed our birthdays, Easter, and even Christmas. Pa missing Christmas was especially hard on Mikey and me. However, Pa was making more money, so there were new clothes for us instead of the Goodwill hand-me-downs, plus I was able to get some things I had been wanting for a long time. In some ways, it was the best years of my childhood. The constant turmoil, so destructive emotionally, was lessened, as was the physical abuse. I was less the anxiety-ridden child that I had been for so long; struggling with never wanting to eat for fear of gagging and throwing up all the time. The normal conflicts with being a girl were starting to crop up, and I was confused and uncertain about being a tomboy all the time. Ma agreed to let me grow my hair long, so with that, combined with wearing the new dresses and skirts I had received because we could finally afford them, I felt feminine. Maybe what my teachers said about me being pretty and a special young lady was true.

One day, when the school nurse came to a special class for the girls to discuss the differences between boys and girls, my mind was drawn back to the bad thing that happened in the barn with Pete. I wanted to know what I should do from somebody I could trust with my secret. Maybe the nurse could understand what I was feeling about being a girl and having that awful thing happen to me. Maybe the nurse could make me understand how to stop the strange and terrifying dreams I had about it happening to me again. I wanted to tell the nurse, but I didn't have the courage. I engaged myself with willful energy in school.

I begged Ma to let me join a softball team, promising I would always get my chores and schoolwork done; Ma finally gave in. I found out quickly how good I could be after just a few short weeks of practice and play. It was a nice reprieve to be able to have fun and play softball with other girls from the area. For many of my classmates and me, this had been our first real attempt at independence and social interactions beyond school. The peer pressures and taunting of one another was all in good fun, and I enjoyed having a place to go, a place that was anywhere other than the dull unrewarding drudgery that was life at home. I had somewhere to hang out, laugh with the other kids my age, and enjoy the camaraderie we shared. I looked forward to those softball games and the competition of winning or losing. This gave me just enough light in my life to keep me looking forward with a glimmer of hope that more of these good days would come, and I could achieve my dreams.

It was during one of those early softball games I found my player's niche as the catcher. I had a full view of the playing field and could see and anticipate the actions and moves of every position and player. I felt empowered as the catcher, having the larger measure of command and control of all that was before me on the playing field. Guiding the pitcher and the team with my ever-increasing skills and perception, diminished the feeling of inadequacy I so often felt. Playing catcher was cool, and fortunately, no one ever lost their hold on the bat and hit me by accident.

During one of the more memorable intense games playing against our most feared rival team, I proved my worth in a closely contested matchup with a very skillful play. I was watching the runner from the other team who was on first base subtlety hiding her intent to steal second, I anticipated a split second ahead of her dash and signaled the pitcher, Denise, with a slight nod. The runner, unwisely, went for the steal. I executed with prowess, a play interception with a shout, "Runner!" As Denise pulled back the ball, she turned and threw to the second baseman, Brittany, who snatched the ball in mid-air and astonished the runner with a big surprise tag. With the inning over, my crucial play changed the direction of the game. The whole team jumped for joy and exchanged ample high fives knowing a vital play had been keenly orchestrated by their catcher. It was certainly exhilarating for me when the coach was telling everyone what a great job had been done by all. Coach Bob said, "Well done Sweetpeas! You are all fantastic! Now, let's go out there and win this game!"

I was up to bat next; I was an okay batter, and the team needed a run. Nervously, I walk to the plate, and I scuff-kicked it while raising the bat in position, looking out at the pitcher, and give her a slow, self-assured nod. The pitcher wound up and sent an explosive fastball towards the plate, and I tracked its flight like a slow-motion paper airplane. I swung the bat down and out to intercept the little white dot and felt a firm collision as my arms push the bat through a slashing arc that propelled the ball up and away, beyond the unsuspecting outfielders playing up close because they weren't expecting me to slam a home run. As I dropped the bat and began my run toward first base, I could see from the corner of my eye the fielders were still running out after the ball; I had sent almost to the fence. I didn't look again at anything but the bases locked firmly in my line of sight – first, then second, then third – then suddenly home plate was right in front of me. The catcher, standing stoically in my path, with an empty glove. In near disbelief, I saw her step aside still holding an empty glove, then I looked down to make sure my foot touched the plate. I knew it was the fastest I had ever run the baseline, and the delight filled my soul, unlike anything I had ever experienced. I had done what I thought not possible and I felt so alive! This day was my special day, and it filled me with joy. It was rewarding to know that the long hours of practice actually increased my skill and value as a team member. I was content that the feeling was worth working for, and I would hope to find it again and again and again. I became even more proactive and I always looked forward to going to practice and hanging out with my friends. Some weeks we would win and some weeks we would lose a good tight game, but playing was all that really mattered to me. Coach Bob was always encouraging the team with his words, "Having Fun, win or lose, that was all that mattered." Everyone on the team tried to live by those words of wisdom from the coach. To have fun and enjoy the moment.

When the social interactions of baseball that had buoyed my spirits, came to an end, I quickly became despondent. I had made a couple of friends that I would see at school or occasionally in the park nearby, but they were not enough to fill the void I felt. I still needed to be anywhere other than home, so I explored other sports I could get into until baseball season started up again. Sadly, every group activity I found required me to be driven to and picked up from at times that weren't convenient to Ma. She had more important things to do than worrying about my needs for friends and companionship. I lost the desire to fight with Ma and ultimately settled on competitive swimming because it posed the least amount of transportation conflict for Ma.

I joined the Tombstone Swim Club that practiced at the YMCA building located only a few blocks detour off Ma's regular route to and from work. The facility had two pools, a smaller, shallow one for regular swimming and lessons, and a bigger, deeper, regulation size, competition pool. After three weeks of twice-weekly basic group swimming lessons in the small pool, I was advanced to competitive swimmer status and started competition training in the big pool. Though it was a very solitary sport, I adapted quickly, and the quiet and solitude of it fit me very well.

I soon believed I was a natural-born fish, and I loved being in the pool. The butterfly stroke was my favorite and one of the hardest strokes to swim. My swim Coach, Ms. Butler, really helped on those days when I needed someone to inspire me and assure me I was doing well. The competition training sessions required a new kind of discipline in order to focus mind and body to work together, and I perfected the techniques with long hours of independent practice. I discovered an inner peace in the water I had not known before. The quiet sounds under the water, hearing only my own breathing as I swam lap after lap, was like medicine for my soul.

I enjoyed the sights and sounds of swim meets, too. I remember the rhythmic splashing sounds of the water as each stroke was taken and the sound of other swimmers splashing water on either side of me. I could hear the pulsing sound of my own heartbeat as I glided through the pale-blue cocoon which made me feel like I was in my own special world. I was a fierce competitor in the water with my quick, furtive glances as I gauged my opponent's position while I pushed my body to stay ahead of them. I followed my sure instincts, knowing that if I could make that last turn and come off the wall precisely right, I just might win. Taking a long deep breath as I go into the last turn, flipping over and pushing hard off the wall, gliding out as far as I could before coming up for air, I would be just ahead of my toughest rival April, in the next lane over. The wall on the other end of the pool would be closing in quickly as I kicked as hard as I could. With one more stroke, I would touch the wall and come up out of the water only to realize I had won.

Oh my God, I did it! That was all I could think. I was so sure the girl next to me was going to get to the wall first. Nevertheless, I had touched the wall a few seconds ahead of April and the win was mine. It was the best feeling in the world, even more than that home run.

The water was the one and only place I truly ever felt safe and sure of myself. I had pushed myself hard and proven I could excel, and it kept me motivated. The discipline required to constantly improve my performance meant training my mind and body to go a little farther, a little longer, and a little faster, in every session. Each session required strength training, lifting weights, and many practice hours. Strenuous and physically challenging, my reward for the relentless pursuit of better and faster had me ready to go semi-pro much sooner than my coaches initially expected, and I was fast-tracked to go to Nationals in my first year. Hard work and dedication had really paid off, and everything seemed to be getting better all around me.

I tried roller-skating on a whim and found I had the balance and endurance that I learned in swimming to make me a skillful skater very quickly. Both sports were competitive and required much solitary training to excel. Teamwork was required, yet each allowed and often required, a high degree of individuality at the same time. The competitive nature of both sports was appealing, and my successes fueled the confidence I had been lacking for so long. Speed skating was something I quickly found I could enjoy, and by then I became pretty much a jock with the hopes of using my talent and education to find a new place in life. Occasionally, I would pray that all the bad that I experienced was just a horrible dream. I spent four years swimming competitively, as well as regularly going to my skate club. As a side note, if you look at the team picture of the girls' roller skate team that performed at the Kennedy Space Center's 1976 Bicentennial Salute – you will see a happy me. Maybe that was why the dreams of the sandy beaches of South Florida played over and over in my mind. I was proud of being a part of the team that won the honor to travel to Florida to perform for those astronauts that were brave enough to travel into space. We saluted their bravery, personal risk, dedication, and commitment; traveling into the unknown, into the cold darkness of space to make our world a more informed place to live. Their bravery was what I hoped I could one day find in myself and live a happy life filled with strength and courage.

I was twelve the next time the evil, called Pete, cornered me in the same barn during a party the family was having. The old barn, with the pleasant, earthy smell of baled hay and horses that I enjoyed feeding apples and carrots too had become my safe haven after the traumatic event from years earlier dimmed.

It was my place to hide. I had gone out there to find some quiet and relief from the loud drunkenness of the party because I truly hated all the violence they produced. No matter how many broken noses or black eyes occurred, the males, and sometimes the females, were always up for yet another excuse to indulge in a showing of dominance or superiority. With my eyes closed as the loud music played across the field, I didn't hear Pete come into the barn. I had been lying peacefully on a bale of hay, just daydreaming of all the beautiful things I hoped to have one day. Dreaming of my new life far away from here, of that loving place that I knew must exist somewhere, and I desperately wanted to find it; I knew this place would never give me the peace I wanted and needed. Unfortunately, Pete had other things on his deranged mind. This time I would not escape the brutal attack he had been planning, for years. This time, I was going to know what boys do to girls, especially, if you say "NO".

Quietly, he slithered up behind me, ready to inflict the punishment he had been planning for me, the little bitch who had avoided him for too long now. I had been careful over these last years to avoid Pete whenever his family would come to town to join in on the fun, but today I would not be so fortunate. He was going to show his male dominance, the struggle all of the men had, this thing that had to be proven over and over again. Power and control always had to be possessed, and he was going to prove it to me today.

Pete outweighed me by 100 pounds, so he was able to pin me down easily and pull off my panties from under my purple sundress. He pushed my legs apart and slid his body between them, laying his arm heavy across my chest. The places he was touching felt okay and I liked it. Except for wait, 'No... this is wrong', I hear myself say. Frantically, I fight to get free, I scream and he laughs, Pete grabs my tender boobs and it hurts. Twisting and turning to get out from beneath him, struggling and pounding on his back hard with my fists, but he was too strong for me. Fighting with all I had, I thought if I could kick him one time in the leg that I can get away, but it was not enough. Screaming louder, I realize no one can hear me as Pete punched me in the face and then grabbed my legs. As he pulled me to him, he slammed his hard thing inside me, making me choke at the feeling. I felt like the wind was knocked out of me. I wanted to scream, but all his weight on my small frame prevented me. This vile man-child stole my virginity and my innocence forever. Mean, ugly, and extremely brutal, little more than a mindless act of a dog in heat, Pete forced permanent darkness into a heart and mind and stole away precious light from a tender young soul. My trusting female innocence was forever lost to an ugly Rape.

When Pete was done, obviously so very proud of himself, he declared with bravado, "Got me another cherry!" Bloody and in terrible pain, I wanted to cry but instead lay motionless, barely breathing, fearing more ugly hurt might be coming from him. He glared down with a smirk and laughed at me; with a forceful growl, he reminded me that I had better not tell a soul, or I would get some more of his manhood real quick. I knew he meant it. The evil that was standing over me made me feel small and lost. I was bewildered because family, I thought, was supposed to protect one another, but he had instead done just the opposite and without mercy.

How could Pete do such a thing and why? I ask myself. Why would he do such a thing to me? Still reeling from this latest attack. I never told anyone about what he had done to me four years ago, and now, who would ever believe me about what just happened?

Laying there covered in my own blood, I cried out, "God help me!"

When I can cry no more, I slowly raised myself up from the hay and looked around the barn for something to deal with the blood on my privates and my legs. Finding an old t-shirt left behind by one of the farmhands, I begin to clean myself up, embarrassed and unsure of what just happened, but knowing deep inside that I have to get away from Tombstone. This place was not safe, it never was and it never will be. But how could I escape? I was barely a teenager, and who would want to help me run away from here? I felt so helpless and lost. I cried out in frustration and sadness…"Why God? I pray and go to church. God if you really are there, please show me a better way. Help me learn to follow your path so that I can love myself, Lord, as you Love me. Amen." I had been in the barn alone where I was not supposed to be, that's what they would say. I was a bad girl and had disobeyed my parents' warnings. They would not want to believe such an ugly thing happened, justifying that "Cousin Pete isn't like that, and he would never do such a thing!" That was just the way it was with the Baker clan; my dilemma was real and without a solution. Knowing I couldn't say anything to anyone, not even my Aunt Hazel, I told no one.

So, life just moved on in this horror show. Days and nights were repetitious toil and disappointment; the same ominous arguments and fights Ma and Pa engaged in left Mikey and I always in fear and emotionally isolated. Home was a dangerous place to be and school a place to hide for a precious few hours a day. Saturdays and Sundays were only occasionally quiet and calm when Pa was away trucking and Ma was working in town or visiting with friends, but the clan still gathered regularly at the Baker's home with new players joining for the social combat they enjoyed.

I was stuck in an emotionally harsh, unforgiving environment and desperately needed some way to escape the destruction playing out in my life. I thought, sometimes, about that magic elixir the clan is always drinking and wondered if maybe it will help soothe the torment I feel inside. The days and nights of anguish and hopelessness became weeks, months, and lost years, but as always… I prayed. God was not far away, and I knew that if I followed His plan, I would be saved from this wretched existence I was currently living in.

3

ANYWHERE BUT HOME

Prayer kept my hopes alive. Each and every night I would pray. I reminded God that I worked hard to be a good girl, I promised I would take care of Mikey better, and that I was still trying at school every day to keep my grades up to the high standards I had set for myself. I reminded Him that I excelled in sports and made friends with other girls and they thought I was a good friend and a good teammate. The harsh feelings of despair quieted slowly and I could smile because that little voice spoke to me and said: "Don't forget I hear you and see you all the time, even in the dark." I would drift away each night holding onto the hand of God, I found glimmers of hope in the solitude when memories of school, the pool, and the skating arena filtered into my mind.

I worked hard to excel at anything that was not the family norm, all the while hearing that guiding voice inside my heart quietly telling me to trust in what I was doing and everything would be okay. I obeyed that voice and followed through as my faith pushed and pulled me along to succeed. Occasionally, I would remember those little encouraging talks about God with Auntie or Grandma, and I would feel encouraged to keep going. Time spent at home remained emotionally empty, and my faith and prayer were not strong enough to overcome the angst and despair I felt day in and day out. Was I destined for something more than the vicious cycle of endless drinking and fighting my family was immersed in?

On a particularly dark and rainy day on which Pa was away trucking and Ma was off visiting friends somewhere, I was dutifully doing my household chores like the good little slave girl I was when I accidentally knocked a bottle of liquor from the counter and it crashed to the floor. I fearfully picked it up hoping to God it wasn't broken or I would be in terrible trouble. I held it up and saw it wasn't, so as I was reaching to put it in the cupboard my curiosity stopped me; I examined the bottle more closely, and read "VODKA, *80 Proof" I decided I had to test the firewater myself; maybe I could understand why they all loved to drink it and get crazy and angry.

Surprisingly, I did not like that first drink much; just a little sip of the clear liquid was hot and burned my throat. It was funny how it made my stomach feel warm and tingling after I took another sip. A few more little drinks from the bottle and my head was feeling the same warm sensation and I felt like it was somewhat alright, and I began to smile. I held the bottle for a long moment staring at it before putting it carefully away in the cupboard. Maybe it wasn't so bad after all. Maybe I was wrong and the feeling I was having about everything right now was okay. Maybe the firewater wasn't bad for everybody because I felt alright, and I didn't want to fight with anybody at all.

Who would tell me that I should stop right there?
Right now!
A simple accident had opened the door to a world I surely wasn't ready for. The days ahead after the fateful first taste of

firewater would bring new and unexpected pressures and with them the subtle changes in my thinking I wasn't aware of and certainly wouldn't understand. Small things at first, and then beneath the surface the fears and stresses I had learned to cope with grew ever more present and ever larger.

Cousin Pete and his pals became a lurking menace to my well-being. After moving closer to the Baker homestead with his family, Pete would regularly make his way over to the Bakers invited or not. At his first appearance, I hid in my bedroom until he was gone. Just the sight of him had made my skin crawl and my stomach so tied in knots I couldn't eat any dinner that night. He came again just a few days later with what would be his most favored pretext – to help Pa with his truck or to work on the homestead doing something that Pa might need his help doing. However, he knew how rarely Pa was home, so the sly look he gave me when I saw him easily revealed what was really on his mind. If Pa wasn't there when he showed up, he would volunteer to do anything that Ma wanted doing. It didn't matter what it was; he was all too happy to help out 'family'.

I knew different from his very next surprise visit because neither Pa nor Ma was home, but he wanted to come in and wait for them anyway. I told him he couldn't stay, and he walked away saying, "I'll be back Tiffany, I'll be back to see you again." I knew all too well he would keep trying to get at me again until he succeeded. The constant fear I lived in from his earlier assaults was now increased by the knowledge that another attack could come at any time. I would have to be on guard at all times. I was so frustrated with the fact that I had nowhere to go to escape his presence; he was so close and so often right in my face. Even worse, Pete would bring his friends around as often as he could when Pa was there just to help Pa around the house, as he would say, but it was mostly to intimidate me and impress his friends with whatever he was telling them. It made me sick just the sight of him and knowing he had probably bragged to them about 'getting my cherry' so I did my best to ignore all the looks or sly remarks they made when nobody but me could hear them say 'how pretty I was getting' or 'what they would like to do to me out there in the big ole barn'.

Almost every visit by Pete forced me to relive all those horrible memories in the barn. There seemed to be nothing I could do to stop my horrible anguish, but one day I went in search of that bottle of liquor to feel, for a little while, that warm tingling feeling that made me feel okay and not angry and afraid. I found a half-full bottle and a little shot glass in the cupboard went to my room and started sipping the hot, fiery liquid. I poured the glass fully and drank it down several times until the warm feeling began changing my world from fear and anger to fuzzy and funny. I sat on the bed trying to hold the bottle and the glass still in my shaking hands and started to cry.

I only wanted a better life without all this craziness going on around me. I couldn't hold back the despair in my heart or the sobbing roaring from my soul. I only wanted little things. To have friends, be outgoing, happy, and funny, but I was forced to be at home all the time with people who only wanted to argue and fight. Why God, Why? I was left alone so often with sneaky Pete right down the road waiting with his friends to drag me into the barn and hurt me over and over and maybe kill me. Why? I was always afraid now. I was so shy and felt so awkward when I was around my friends and other people away from home. Even at school, I was more afraid of things every day, and I was becoming a loner and didn't want to be.

Why does this have to happen to me? Why God, why?

My room began spinning me around violently as the bottle and glass fell from my hands and darkness descended over me.

I awoke in severe pain that I had never known before. Everything hurt, and my throat was dry, and I felt so sick to my stomach. I got up from the bed, fell immediately from being so dizzy and shaky, and threw up. Slowly, I crawled in the darkness to the bathroom to get some water and wash myself up. It was horrible how I felt.

I now felt exactly what I had only seen so often from my family when they got drunk and slept in the bathroom puking all night. I don't want to do this again I heard myself say over and over. It was my first-hand glimpse into the powerful, dark forces hidden in a bottle of vodka.

I was reminded of those memories that had brought about my first attempt at escaping this world and the actions that almost ended my life; I knew it was not going to get any better here. There was too much missing.

Teenage fun had been a long-awaited event for me. I did the very best I could at trying to just be a kid, of wanting to have fun, play sports, and go to school to learn – all those things kids are supposed to do. I wanted to chill down at the lake while hanging out with the few friends and cousins I felt I could trust. Unfortunately, these events were precious to me because they were so rare. Days at the lake, swinging from the rope out over the water or jumping off the dock laughing and drinking, made me feel good and were great fun. As everyone paired up with their boyfriends and snuggled close near the campfire trying to warm up after a day in the lake, the stars overhead always left me dreaming of a better life that just wasn't happening for me now.

"Why do I feel so alone" was a question I couldn't answer?

"Help me please", I hear myself say, think, someone please help.

My lack of self-esteem and more despair ever-present, I can only observe as others laugh and enjoy life the way I'd hoped to one day. For now, however, there seemed to be only this place of desert plains, drinking, and the games that went along with it. I was valiantly trying to make a difference in my own life and find a way to escape the destructive environment I hated, but by myself, I was failing. I could barely concentrate on anything. My schoolwork was beginning to show my weakened resolve to excel because I was drinking a little more each day and often was near being drunk in a steady downward spiral. Drinking was my only means to just forget the agonizing world I lived in. All my drive from the commitment and determination I held onto was being drained drop by drop and my dreams shattered by the constant stress and abuse. This was no life for a young teenager. Life had to have more I believed, there just had to be more, and with that little bit of hope still echoing inside and pushing me along, the answer appeared right in front of me.

I never stopped praying for God to show me a way out of the dark place I was trapped in. How was I going to get there? When could it or would it happen? One day while wandering aimlessly through town after Ma dropped me off early in the morning to go window shopping, as Ma called it, "in the twinkling of an eye" as it's said, I spot it, a sign at the local diner.

 HELP WANTED... Dishwasher Needed!!!

I was scared. This grown-up thing I was about to do at fourteen was a big step into the adult world I wanted to be part of. Taking a giant leap of faith, I stiffly stepped through the door into Bell's Diner to ask about the help wanted sign posted in the window. The smells of old grease and stale coffee immediately hit me and gave my already queasy stomach another jolt.

I saw an apron wrapped around the waist of a middle-aged waitress who was coming over to greet me. "Have a seat anywhere you want," the waitress says, thinking I was just another hungry customer.

"I want to speak to the manager if I could please," I tell her. "Okay. I will go tell him. Have a seat; it might be a couple of minutes," she replies. I slide into a booth close to the door to wait for the manager. I was really nervous but wanted more than anything to get away from all the conflicts at home, and this was going to be some part of that if I could get the job. I could only hope whomever I was waiting for would give me a chance to prove I was a good worker and would allow me to have a job here.

I saw a tall, slightly bald, heavyset man with a stained white, full-body apron come around the end of the sit-down counter and amble towards me. Though I was sitting, I could see and sense as he was coming towards me with a familiar hard and critical appraisal. Something instinctual sent a pulse-racing thru my mind and made my stomach tighten. I smiled at him with my best adult-like smile as he said to me, "What do you need?"

Perfunctory and slightly menacing, without even the smallest of a "How may I help you?" I sensed this would be an ominously familiar encounter. He was giving me that same calculating look Pete and his pals were always giving me – cold and cruel. I was sadly familiar enough now with that look from a man to know what it meant, and I shivered slightly before speaking a word.

"I was wondering about the dishwasher job," I answered steadily. "I want to work and I can wash dishes really well," I said and pleaded my case in a shy, quiet voice. I sat quietly, feeling hopeful, and did not resist his eyes looking into mine with a hard stare that said; "I am the boss and you will do what I tell you to do little girl." After a long wait when he probably expected me to surrender my nerve, he caved in and spoke up, "Well, I need you 3 hours a night during the busy dinner rush. Minimum wage is all I can pay you".

"Oh, that's perfect," I said with a big smile lighting up my face.

"Okay then, I will see you tomorrow," he said. I slid myself out of the booth in one swift, happy movement, skipped through the door and took off in a run to tell Ma that I had a job. All I needed was Ma to sign the school/work release form and file it with the school board for approval, so I could legally work at fourteen. When I arrived, breathless and beaming, at home to tell Ma I had gotten a real job at Bell's Diner, Ma was all too happy to hear it and did not hesitate to sign at all. She announced, she knew both where the Diner was and the gruff man who owned it, as he had cooked her meals the few times she had eaten there. My whole life was going to change, and now I would be doing more than housework and getting yelled at all the time. I overheard Ma make a hurtful little remark to the clerk at the school board office about me being in the way at home all the time which made me certain that Ma was more than happy for me to be out of sight and out of mind.

Bell's was the only place to eat that was easily accessible from the main state highway a half-mile away. A big, old, blue and white, billboard sign on the highway stated.

GOOD FOOD — *EAT AT* — BELL'S DINER   > NEXT EXIT

There were a couple of other local places to eat, but they were another mile deeper into Tombstone, Texas on a pot-holed, two-lane road, and there was no place for the truckers to park their big-rigs. Those restaurants were never very busy either because even the locals didn't frequent them, so Bell's was the best option for a young girl to find work. For me, Bell's was a chance to work and make a little money of my own to spend, and I was certain I was ready to make my own way and be an adult. It was just the start I needed. Unfortunately, later on, I would realize it was not the direction I should have chosen, had there been other choices.

This is where my life takes a turn down a new road. Good or Bad, something had to change, and I was the only one that could make it happen. The school was the only place I could be my true competitive self. Aside from my swimming and skating, I knew it made me smarter and better at a lot of things. I was determined to advance my life to be disciplined in my school work and stop drinking so much. With my passion for mechanics and my math abilities strong, I began to excel in school again. I was still intoxicated way too often, but regardless, I did the work in front of me. I did not see Pete and his friends as often, and some of the everyday worries lessened in his absence. There were fewer arguments and fights on the homefront because it seemed Pa was on the road trucking more than he was at home. I was able to find a degree of calm that I had long been searching for.

On the flip side, the calm I had found was, in a way, unsettling because I began to believe no one was there for me. The insecure, self-destructive side of my personality emerged rapidly when I drank the vodka, which had become my favorite escape from boredom.

Did the abuse from my childhood have an impact on me as a teenager trying to deal with the hormones that come with adolescence? Were the unknowns and the emotional highs and lows that are a natural part of this maturing process making me more vulnerable to feeling disliked or possibly being loved at all? Was the stress of being a mother and caretaker for Mikey most of my life keeping me from feeling independent and confident in myself? Maybe working and being around people could change it. I showed up early for my first day of work, for training, as the manager called it. I was super excited, believing a Higher Power was leading me and God had answered my prayers. The other dishwasher/busboy showed me the procedures, and I quickly learned how to manage the steady flow of dishes from the kitchen to the customers' table and back to the kitchen again. There were huge pots and oversize pans in the mix, too. Also, I had to go out to the dining room to help the waitresses with clearing the tables when they got behind. When the big dinner-time rush was over, I had to help out with cleaning the booths, floors, and whatever other work needed to be done. Often I would cringe thinking about my workplace environment – the wet, slimy floors, grungy stove, and endless piles of heavy ceramic dishes I had to handle, but I knew it was my best chance of escape.

I would repeat daily, "Lord I know you brought me here, for

a reason. Please help me learn this job, and I'll be the best dishwasher I can possibly be." And I did, or rather, He did, or was it both? I had found my hidden strength. My initiative was my special power – a willingness to learn on my own, to seek for myself and find what worked, and to know and understand how to get what I wanted and needed. With initiative and determination, I was less susceptible to the deforming pressures around me. However, there was one small problem, alcohol. I was hiding the fact I was now drinking daily. I spent almost all of my waking hours in a state of intoxication. Alcohol was soothing the emotional pain inside, and I was starting to realize and understand why many of those around me did the same. It softened the emotional ache of depression. There was, however, a more dangerous aspect I knew practically nothing about.

Natural curiosity after the Pete experience made me ponder the mysteries about sex. I learned a few things from some talkative female classmates, as well as I observed what the older cousins and some of the grown-ups did at the clan gatherings, not to mention hearing some sexual expressions down at the lake coming from the bushes when no one knew anyone was there or maybe didn't care that anyone was. I casually learned how to identify that look of sexual interest and saw some part of the 'dance' that usually followed. I saw how it worked and quickly learned how to exploit it. If I just smiled at a man with a flirty smile and turned on my girlish charm, I usually got what I wanted which, for me, was a generous tip. I was overly eager, with cause, to set the stage with my womanhood and explore the way out of this horrible place I was trapped in. Arrogant, immature, teenage bravado at its destructive best put my moral soul on the menu with a price, and worse yet, with only a child's understanding of its value and its cost.

I liked my job; it was just a messy job at times, but not a hard job. When I was able to work with the customers at the counter and in the dining room, I actually liked it a lot. The customers all seemed to like me and most of them left me good tips. I did not really like Donald very much, but he was my boss, so I always did whatever he said the best I could. He was kind of a nasty man; he did not shave every day or keep his hair combed, and many days I could smell the whiskey he sipped every few hours from the bottle he kept in the food pantry. He wore the same smelly clothes every day underneath his big wrap-around cooking apron. He was often mean and sarcastic, pointing out when I did not do something exactly the way he said and asking me if I would ever learn to do it right. Sometimes, the diner would be packed, and customers would come in and be waiting for a place to sit, when he would shout at me from behind the kitchen counter window, "Hurry up! Stop talking so much," even when I was hurriedly writing down a customer's order. "Sorry," was all I could say, as I cringed inside and give the customer a smile of apology.

I would always apologize to Donald and tell him I would get it right next time as I went back to the kitchen with dirty dishes or to the window to pick up an order. He usually just glared at me with disdain and grumbled I had better get it right soon. He was mean, but I had a job, and I wanted to keep it. More and more often, and usually, when there were just a few customers sitting at the counter who probably wouldn't notice, I would turn and see Donald staring at me while I was clearing booth tables along the front window wall. I had to lean way over to reach the back of the table to clear it off along with resetting the little wire baskets of salt & pepper, Sweet-N-Low, and the menu holders. The little black uniform dress that Donald's other waitress, Marley, had gotten for me to wear was really too short than what I would normally wear, but Marley said it looked good on me, and so I wore it. When I leaned and stretched way over, it showed more of my legs and pulled tighter on my buttocks than I wanted, and I was always careful about it. I pretty much knew this was why Donald would stare at me, and it made me afraid some days of what he would say, or even do if I was not careful about it when nobody else was around.

I struggled to get my grades back up so I could work, as it was a requirement for the privilege. Doing okay in school, again, I began to search for who I was supposed to be and to find my identity of who I wanted to be when I grew up. That was what school is all about, right? Maybe even finding a boyfriend and some peace in my life? I found true performance pleasure in my Pre-Engineering class when I learned to scale the designs on my paper, engineering those plans, T-square, and angles – making it all come to life. I really missed the good 'ole days of semi-leisure and fun playing softball or swimming laps in the pool, but I worked hard at the necessary academics to graduate while keeping my job and making a little money, so I could have a sense of freedom and independence.

I was mostly happy, but only because I was busy with school and work, and I missed my friends to share my life events with on a regular basis. Although it was tough, I held fast to the belief that if I worked hard enough, my life would get better, and one day I could buy a car and drive off happily into the sunset to live a wonderful new life. The dream seemed elusive, and youthful impatience was causing serious depression and loneliness in a never-ending vicious cycle.

Walking from school on my way to work one sunny afternoon, Kent, a boy I had seen at school, walked up to me with a funny smile on his face. He said "hello" and I immediately felt his friendly demeanor was real and I smiled back at him with a soft "hello."

He asks, "Tiff have you ever tried weed?" Looking at him with a quizzical look I said, "No, what's Weed?" Kent laughed and asked, "Want to try some?" When I didn't say 'no' he said, "Follow me."

We walked between two buildings and Kent lit up the joint he was holding. He breathed in, coughed, laughed, and passed it to me, asking me again if I wanted to try it.

I hesitantly replied, "*Okay*," and take it. As I breathed in the smoke, I immediately felt like everything was spinning, and yet I was in a carefree haze that made me smile. This is my first peer pressure encounter and it was not going to have a happy conclusion.

All though, I did like this new thing called weed; isn't that what he called it?

After a few moments, I feel the blurry, fuzzy feeling clear just a bit. "Cool, I like that. Where can I get some?" I asked Kent, wanting to add this new dimension to my daily escape. And for me, it was as easy as that.

I fell into the peer pressure trap, the same place so many of us fall into, believing, well... if they're doing it, I guess I should too. Unfortunately, so many of us, myself included, are not mature enough to contemplate any consequences down the road as teenage curiosity and the urges of independence push and pull us along.

Kent moves in swiftly for a kiss and says, "I'll get you some, but you have to do what I want." A jarring flashback to Pete hits me, and my mind revolted in disgust. "No! Go away" I screamed. The feeling of betrayal crushes me like a huge rock dropping on my foot. All men are like Pete, and why do they only seem to want to do those sex things with me? Why, Lord, are boys like that? They all seem the same? Why, I wonder, couldn't he just like me for me?

I had a new and serious problem because I really liked the feeling of this 'weed' and had to find a supplier. I began asking around the school the few kids that I could trust about who was holding some weed. I believed it should not be too hard to get because I had been buying Rum for a while from Ben at the local liquor store. Yes, I was underage, and he knew, but I was persuasive with my fledgling feminine wiles, and after several attempts, he gave in to me; it would be our little secret. I knew he enjoyed the little game we were playing, and we would joke about how he might like to have a drink with me one day when I got out of school. I knew exactly what he really wanted, so I would always laugh and say, "Well... maybe one day we can do that when I don't have homework or work, which I need to get to now," as I would quickly exit out the door of his store with the rum he sold me.

I got that weed connection a few days later. It was where my first real sense of freedom and adult independence came into play, having my own money to buy drugs and alcohol. Along with buying new clothes and shoes with the money my job was providing me, I even started thinking about buying my own car. I would have to start saving some of my paychecks if I was going to get my own car when I turned sixteen. Taking care of me meant planning ahead and being ready when the day came that I was old enough to leave Tombstone behind to make my own way in the world.

I met up with my first drug dealer, Ralph, a boy two grades ahead of me at school, and bought another ticket to addiction. A small amount of weed and a small bottle of Rum or Vodka lasted a few weeks when I first started, indulging the highs and the lows that followed when I ran out of either or both. It was only a short time later, that I made sure I always had both on hand. I began indulging myself every day and every night with both. Soon, I was drinking before school and then smoking weed before I left school for work in the girl's bathroom or outside in the cover of the stairwell pillars. School quickly became just a place to be away from home, and work became a place to make the money I needed to support my highs. I became more isolated by choice, preferring to drink and drug alone at home or wherever I could be where no one could observe me or interfere with what I wanted to do. I was barely functional most days but virtually unaware that others noticed my erratic attitude and behavior. My life was becoming a blur as I escaped my emotional pain, and the dullness of steady alcohol and drug use created a new kind of anguish as I became more distrustful and outright angry with anyone who interfered with my near-constant high.

The path of *self-destruction* by way of drugs and alcohol had firmly set in.

Falsely believing the allusion that I was different, and what I was doing really wasn't causing me harm, I put up a protective wall against any necessity or reason to quit drinking and smoking. I always felt a protective spirit was close, something good was always guiding me, and my prayers were being answered. The little girl, still clinging to the faith of constant guidance from God, became numb and deaf to the small voice when the unchecked freewill of my youthful, immature flesh was empowered by mind-altering mood-shifting substances. I was spiraling out of control, and I fought the moments of critical self-reflection that naturally occurred when the drink and drugs dropped me unexpectedly to the floor after serious and excessive overindulgence. Was there anyone or any way to save me from the destructive course I was following? Was there anyone who could pull me back from the precipice? Will I get lost as so many other young people in the world do, left to their own devices and self-guidance?

I held onto my dreams and hopes of a happy, fulfilling life and daydreaming about finding a good man who would love me and care for me. I saw myself with him, as we strolled along the boardwalk, holding hands in a big city or enjoying a nice candlelight dinner. These dreams were the real substance that made me smile, believing love would find me, and I could be who I was meant to be. Loving and being loved was the foundation of hope that I was building all my dreams on. However, my hard-edged, limited understanding of male and female relationships would weaken my foundation permanently, without warning, when I heard the wrong words at the wrong time. I learned that the sexual attacks by Pete destroyed any real hope of making my wedding day special when I overheard a conversation about virginity between two girls sitting next to me in the cafeteria. I was shattered. I knew I had morals and values, but now I falsely believed there was something ugly about me that I could never change and made me unlovable by a good man. Those beautiful things I read about in Cosmo magazine while loitering in the drug store those afternoons when I needed to get out of the heat on my way home from school, were now, perhaps, not to be mine because I was no longer a virgin. The grown-up experiences that were waiting out there on the horizon might actually not be there for me. Those ideas where maybe I would be okay and live a good and beautiful life were growing ever farther from me as I was being engulfed in feelings of shame and guilt. The self-worth, esteem, and fragile self-perceptions that I was building my identity on were crumbling as I felt more and more undeserving of my long-sought-after dreams.

I had been working at the diner for about two years and had become proficient at my job that even my boss begrudgingly admitted I was a valuable employee. On a rainy evening, not long after my shift began, one of my teachers from school stopped in to eat dinner. Ms. Williams had been my math teacher the year before and recognized me when I walked up to ask if I could bring her something to drink.

"Tiffy is that you," Ms. Williams asks. "Yes ma'am, how are you doing tonight?" I answered warmly. "The weather sure is ugly out there tonight, what can I bring for you?" I took her order and hurried off to the kitchen to pour a big bowl of chicken noodle soup and filled a little tin teapot with hot water. I carefully placed a tea bag and lemon wedge on the side of the plate placed all the items on my tray and returned to the table. After assuring Ms. Williams I would be nearby if she needed anything else, I went about my other work clearing the tables as the few other customers remaining finished their meals and departed. I went to check on Ms. Williams after she had finished her soup to ask if she would like more soup or another cup of tea. Ms. Williams thanked me and told me that she had enough, but yes, she would like to talk to me for a few minutes if I could. Looking to see if my boss was peering through the kitchen service window, I sat down across from my old teacher and smiled, saying to her that it was nice to see her again.

Ms. William looked at me with such warmth and said; "You know, Tiffy, you were one of my brightest students last year. I hope that you are doing okay and things have gotten a bit better for you. Some of the other teachers around the school also have commented about how you seem to be struggling, and it is such a shame because you have enormous potential." I almost busted out crying as a lump formed in my throat, but a customer came through the door just on cue, and I excused myself and quickly got up from the table. I thanked Ms. Williams for the kind words and asking her if she cared for any dessert; she didn't, so I left her the check and went back to my duties.

A few nights later, I had noticed a trucker watching me and decided I was going to try something. With a subtle female hip swagger, I walked past him carrying a rack of coffee cups to put out front and glanced at him with my best flirting smile. He understood my intent, and the second time I walked past his table he asked, "Hey, what's your name?"

"Tiffany. Can I get you something, Sir?" I asked beaming. "Yes, thanks, just some coffee. My name is JR," he replied. I returned with the coffee pot, slowly filled his cup, and said, "It's a pleasure to meet you JR." He lingered drinking his coffee for most of an hour as I dutifully kept his cup full accompanied by a big smile each time I went to his table. He departed while I was in the kitchen for a few moments, but when I went to his empty table, I found a tip more than double what most truckers would give me. Maybe my smile did work magic, I thought, smiling to myself.

As the weeks passed, JR would come to the Diner, and we would talk a few brief moments while he was there. I could tell every time I walked by him that he was watching me with great interest. A friendship grew between us; this older guy seemed to like me and it gave me a happy feeling that someone was noticing me, but I was just a little bit apprehensive, so I guarded my fragile emotions. Nevertheless, steadily with the hormones of a teenager and the mildly intoxicated state I was usually in, romantic intrigue took its natural course. I began to think maybe life was finally going to get better, that maybe JR could be my Prince Charming. With a steady supply of cute smiles or coy glances when he was at the Diner, I began directing my ambitions toward escaping Tombstone with my new Prince leading the way. A fairy tale dream, like one of those stories Aunt Hazel read to me all those years ago, had formed in my mind with JR playing a major role.

One night while he was sitting in the diner having his coffee and watching me, JR asked, "Tiffy have you ever gone for a ride in a Big Rig?" Laughing, I say, "No, of course not. Do you own one of those trucks out there?" I had never actually ridden in Pa's truck because he said it wasn't a place for kids. Not really knowing what JR was thinking about me other than that I had gotten him interested in me as a girl, or better yet, the woman I believed I now had become, I threw all caution into the wind, said; "But it might be really cool." "Yes it would, and I am sure you would like it. I own that red Freightliner out there," JR beamed. Tiffany Rose Baker did not really know where that ride would take her or what jeopardy she had thrust herself into. Long, pent-up desires to know the kind of love she had dreamed of so often, the hormones of a teenage girl, and the desire to leave behind her tumultuous life put her into the passenger's seat of that truck without thinking where the ride would take her.

"Well, how long before you're off work?" JR asked. "I'm off now," I told him with a big excited grin. "Let's go! I love new adventures."

I did not see the gun or the drugs JR had under his seat when he opened the door and boosted me up into the passenger seat of his truck. He closed the door, walked around to the other side, and climbed up into the driver's seat bringing the big rig to life with the low roar of its big diesel engine. It was music to my ears, and I was thrilled to be up high in the seat looking down on the world in front of me. A cold rush running through me, I let my emotions run wild as JR played it cool flipping on some country music, and taxied me down that old, country road heading into the sunset.

The big engine roared, and the dust flew behind us as JR wheeled the truck up and down a maze of farm roads with me smiling, laughing, and making small talk about a truckers' life.

I told him about Pa being a trucker and that I understood a lot already about being out on the road all the time. I beamed broadly as the cactus and tumbleweed flew by and spotted a lot of big Black Angus cattle seemingly looking up to greet me as we drove by on roads I had not ridden on before. Finally, I was entering into that adult world I had been waiting so long for and now felt free to be whoever I want to be. Sitting high up in the passenger's seat of this big truck as it roared down the road while a cute guy who liked me behind the wheel taking me where I wanted to go, everything was looking simple and uncomplicated.

"What's wrong?" I ask JR when he began slowing down the big rig and makes a U-turn at a road sign with an arrow saying Tombstone, thirty-eight miles. I thought we had been having fun. All these weeks of flirting and talking, JR coming in the Diner whenever he came thru town, I thought we had something really special.

"Listen, Tiffy, I've got to get down the road for a while. I have a big load to deliver across the country, and I am already a week behind on my schedule, but I'll be back soon," he said in a pleading way. During another hour of riding, I was trying to make small talk but not feeling the adrenaline high and giddy excitement the brief road trip gave me. I told JR how much I enjoyed the ride in his truck and thanked him for taking me as we pulled back into the lot next to Bell's Diner.

"Wow! That was fun JR; I really had fun," I said. "I enjoyed it, too, Tiffany. It was fun for me with you sitting over there," JR said with a big smile. He climbed down from the cab and came around to open the door and helped get me down from my seat as he repeated that he would be back soon. I walked away from the truck as he climbed back up into the cab and stood to look forlorn as JR pulled out of the lot and drove away with a small piece of my heart. I walked back into the diner and waited for my ride back home wondering if I had done something wrong. I didn't yet know that I had actually done everything right this time.

Heartbroken and puzzled, I watched and waited for days for

JR to return. Weeks passed and still no JR. All I could do was wonder where he was with hopes of seeing him once again and to feel that happy smile inside I always got every time he came to Bell's Diner. I daydreamed often of being able to flirt with him again as he drank coffee and watched me work. I did my work at the diner along with my schoolwork, but without much interest in either. The effects of alcohol and weed increased my depression; my attitude toward everyone around me was more antagonistic than social and friendly. I stayed away from home as much as I could; I was there only to shower, sleep, and change clothes. I performed my school and work routines in a darkening daze, unfortunately, part of my own making. One warm Sunday morning, Grandma stopped by the house after church to see Ma and asked me why I looked so sad. "Grammy," I said, "I just don't understand boys or what they really want from us. Why do they act so weird?" Not wanting to tell Grammy what I was really thinking or ask why boys want sex all the time, I didn't reveal what was really troubling me. "Now listen, Tiff, you don't fret about boys just yet. You're still young, and you will understand in time," She admonished me tenderly. Grammy did not know what I had already learned about boys and sex; unfortunately, I knew far less than I needed to.

I followed Grammy out to the porch to sit in the rocking chairs and talk awhile. I told her about JR coming into the diner and talking to me. I told her that he said he was coming back but hadn't returned. She told me that it would all work out as God planned. I accepted her words with teenage reservation, and after the two of us had a piece of the cake she had brought, I thanked her for our talk and gave her a big hug. Maybe I should have told her what was really on my mind and confided a little in my grandmother, but I didn't and the chance to unburden myself with fateful questions came and went in silence.

A few days later I was surprised when my Pa brought me an old Mustang fixer-upper car for my sixteenth birthday. I was ecstatic with the fulfillment of a long-held hope, and it put some joy in life as it lit up my world. I felt a new happiness that never existed before that day. When he handed me the keys, he said he was sorry for how bad he had always treated me and asked for my forgiveness. I was so excited to have a car and a way to leave this terrible place that forgiving my Pa was easy; the memories of all the pain and bruises were far from my mind. As I ran around my car inspecting the beauty of the old clunker, I said, "Thanks Pa. So what do we need to do to get it running?"

Perhaps, with a certain amount of guilt pushing him to make up for the past, a long-overdue father-daughter relationship emerged between us as I learned the skills of auto mechanics that Pa knew so well. I was an avid learner from the start. As we began the long process and tore apart the engine of that faded evergreen colored 1969 Mustang Fastback with a 302 Boss engine in it, I found a new outlet for some of the anger I felt towards so many things and more than a few people. I fell in love with my new project and was eager to master all I could about all things automotive and did so with flair and humor. I learned a few cuss words as skinned knuckles and rusted parts tested my patience. Wrenching became second nature to me and being called a tomboy went with my newfound love of mechanics because I liked cars and only boys worked on cars. I did not care the slightest what my mother and others said about my unwomanly greasy hands which were a regular complaint at the dinner table. Every day I wasn't working at the diner, I would beg Pa to do some more work with me on my car, or have him explain what was next, so I could continue when he wasn't around. It was exhilarating to dream of feeling the power of the car when I could finally wheel it down those old, dirt roads. I felt pride as I restored life to my most prized possession and my ride to freedom. I loved the feeling of working on my car as Pa and I completed another part of the puzzle. Sadly, the car adventure with my Pa would be the one and only chance I had of ever having a close relationship with him – a man I always tried hard to love and understand. We had fun and would joke around, but there were serious times when he explained why things went together and how things worked. As we progressed with the car, we simultaneously built a close and caring relationship that we both treasured and it always showed. We finished rebuilding the engine and fixed the body with steady effort and long hours. I was ready to see my work come alive. Soon I would enjoy the sound of my car roaring down the road. I had saved money from my work to buy the insurance and tags to make the car and myself, as its driver, legal. The day finally came when all was in place, and I was so nervous that my hands were shaking as I put the key in the ignition ready to give the Mustang its first real road test. Smiling from ear to ear, I looked back at my Pa, turned the key, and heard the engine came alive, and so did I.

"Pa, please take me for a drive down the street," I asked. Pa agreed and climbed into the car as excitement like something I'd never known before overflowed in my heart and mind. Maybe the same excitement would remain in my soul as the big triumph of my dreams come true. Cars would be my first true love, cars, muscle cars to be exact, fast and sleek, flying me down the road with dust trailing behind me. My dream was now a reality; sweet sixteen with a car and a job, I was feeling very hopeful and even somewhat cool about my new life.

Dreams fulfilled often hold surprises and not all of them wanted or good. With my newfound freedom and free will running wild, I drove away from home one night heading to the skating rink by way of a half-pint of rum. Before I even reached the rink, I was so drunk that it was a true miracle I arrived there in one piece. I skated drunk and very high, losing all sense of how I had gotten to the rink and all the work and dedication it took to get there. I had no thought that night about the future or what my unchecked self-indulgence would cost.

I believe God really does protect drunks and fools, as they say. Because a few days later after the drunken drive to the skating rink, I was out drinking and driving again on a hot rainy night after fighting with Ma and ran that Mustang head-on into a cement telephone pole.

Driving way too fast in the rain and taking a hard left turn on that slick pavement, the back of the car fishtailed, sliding right then left. I let go of the wheel and slammed into the pole. The impact pushed the engine block into the firewall of the car with a force of steel against solid concrete that should have killed me.

> Apparently, God had other plans for me, and maybe it was to tell you this Story.

Luckily, I was alive but again without a car only a month after getting one. All those dreams of leaving home and finding a new place to start over were now destroyed and hopes of that place of peace and serenity where I could smile all day and enjoy life were gone. So back to work I go still trying to figure out how I could escape. With my hopes crushed along with my car, I was left wondering if God was still there. I hoped He was because I needed Him to begin my journey to freedom again.

I yearned for anything that could change the direction my life was taking. I was waiting for an answer to my dilemma when a glimmer of hope appeared at the diner. I was justifiably excited the night JR finally showed up after more than a month of being gone. I had a serious crush on him, and my hope of finding someone to share my life with made him a perfect candidate for my wish fulfillment. When I saw him walk through the door, I ran over and greeted him with a happy hug meant to secure his attention.

"Oh, JR, I'm so happy to see you," and gave him a big kiss on the cheek. I looked him in the eye and said; "Oh, JR, please, will you take me with you the next time you leave? I sure want to get out of here." Tired of the small-town life in West Texas and dreaming of having a real boyfriend, JR was my Prince Charming; he would not be abusive like my Pa or most other men I knew. I was desperate for an escape, and he could be the one to take me away. Sixteen, lonely, and naive, I was vulnerable to the well-masked guile of JR along with a couple of his trucker friends, and soon-to-be accomplices, who would all too soon reveal to me the evil that lurks in men's hearts. Even ones that said all the right things and hugged you warmly, would prove to be cold and cruel once the innocence of youth was laid barren and the vibrant flower of womanhood plundered by harsh animal desires. It would be a slow and tortuous path of self-discovery and sorrow before I understood what my youthful, blind trust was about to forfeit; and how much of me would be lost or left behind for good. My intentions of leaving this life behind were for me to have a better life. A life where I felt safe and loved, but this would not happen the way I planned.

Nevertheless, my journey must be told, so that you may truly understand how my addictions led me astray, far into the depths of Hell. These events in my life reveal a part of Tiffany Rose Baker that has been well-hidden and known only to God before now.

What would my life be like if JR and his piercing blue eyes had not walked into the diner that day? How would my life be different if this charming, older guy with the assuring voice had not taken interest in me? A man that knew I was vulnerable and naive. If only someone would have warned me then about the games men play with a woman's heart, I might have avoided what was about to happen. How searching for love on that first, fateful ride in a big truck would begin my one-way road trip to an addiction of a much more destructive kind.

In hindsight, it's pretty easy to know what JR was thinking after the first innocent charade I played with him as I swished my hip and flashed my sweet smile during our earliest meeting at Bell's Diner. To him, I spoke loud and clear about what my intentions were, even if I didn't realize what my non-verbal communication would ultimately lead to. It didn't take much for him to get me into his truck that first time, and he knew it. I made it quite obvious during that brief ride with him that I knew little of anything about the world and people outside the city limits of good, old Tombstone, Texas. I was too young, too emotionally high on my first male infatuation, not to mention high and weak-minded with rum and weed to truly understand the consequences of my actions. In addition, I was so desperate to get away from a home that was toxic in so many ways, yet ironically afforded me some protection from the dangers of the world. For him it was beyond easy to lead me anywhere he wanted me to go. I was a simple, country girl ripe for plucking like a fresh spring chicken, and I honestly thought my luck was too good to be true. In my mind, he was affording me the love and affection I so desperately needed, and I thought he would be the key to climbing out of the downward spiral that alcohol and weed were taking me.

4

CLIMBING UP TO FALL HARD

There was a momentary look of disbelief in JR's eyes while I stood motionless at his table in the diner asking him to take me with him when he left. I was serious about it, and I was ready to run off with him right then, and there, no questions asked. Did I mean now? Incredulous, but without much delay, JR answered, "OK. Sure, Tiff, you can ride with me for a while." I wasn't really sure he would agree to take me, but when he said okay, I felt relief and wanted to flee immediately. I blurted out.

"Let's go! I'm ready to go right now. I can leave right now with you."

"Alright then, okay. I am ready to go, too. Do you need to go pack some things?" Do I need to come to get you somewhere?" he asked. "No, no. I am ready to leave right now! I have some money, and I can buy things I need wherever we go," I eagerly declared.

"Well, okay then. I guess we can go," he replied. I walked back to the kitchen and told my boss I was leaving and wasn't coming back to work anymore, and he could give the money I was still owed to my Ma when she came by sometime. Without looking back, I turned and walked out the door I had come through a few years ago when I saw a sign saying, 'Dishwasher Wanted'. All I saw ahead was my Prince Charming, JR, marrying me very soon, and I would make babies to love and cherish and do all the things I had dreamed of for so long. I was going to live the fairy tales I remembered from Aunt Hazel's stories for real now.

I climbed up into the truck with JR and headed west out of Tombstone, Texas on a hot summer day as the sun was just beginning to set. It was indeed the romantic fairy tale start I had envisioned it would be as we sped down the highway into a sky filled with lingering red and gold colors of a romantic sunset. It was all surreal to me. We had driven in near silence for almost an hour, occasionally making small talk. I was telling JR how excited I was and a lot of the things I wanted to do in all the days ahead. With a lot of nodding and approvals to my proclamations about our future, he drove into the setting sun until almost midnight and announced to me that it was time to stop for the night.

"Okay. I need to go to the bathroom anyway," I said. The adrenaline high I had started out the trip with had settled down some, and I felt brave enough to bring up the subject of weed when I had jumped down out of the truck. "Have you ever smoked weed?" I asked JR. He looked at me and chuckled, "Sure I have. Have you ever smoked a joint yourself?

"Sure. All the time," I replied with a weak tired smile. "Well okay then. I have a little weed in the truck. When you come back from the bathroom we can smoke one then," he said. I went into the restroom and took off the diner apron I was still wearing and used it to wash away the long hours of work and riding of the day. I felt better, but sitting and riding in the darkness had made me tired, but there was still a faint feeling of excitement lingering that was keeping me awake. A little smile formed on my lips knowing a little weed would make the day even better than it had already been. I dropped the wet apron into the wastebasket and walked back out to JR who was waiting by the truck.

I smiled as I approached him and said, "I'm ready. Let's do it," I was really ready to smoke the joint he said he had with him. "I'm ready too little lady, I am totally ready," he said with a very big smile. He lit up the joint and after a big puff passed it to me. I took a long pull on the joint and held the smoke in my lungs as long as I could. I exhaled a big cloud with a few hard coughs and felt its soothing effect begin to make my mind fuzzy and ease up the aches my body felt from the ride. It was way more potent than the usual stuff I had been buying, and the initial rush way more intense. After exchanging the joint a few times and letting the effects take hold I asked, "Are we going to a motel or something now?"

"No, not tonight." He pointed up toward the sixty-inch sleeper of the Freightliner and said, "This is our motel for the night. Climb up and let's get into the sleeper and do what we are both ready to do." It suddenly dawned on me that when I said a few minutes ago that 'I was ready' and 'let's do it' referring to the weed we had just smoked, meant something else in JR's mind. Suddenly, a lot of unexpected fear made my heart beat faster as I climbed up into the cab. I sat down in the seat and looked around behind me and into the sleeper part. I remembered Pa telling me he slept in the sleeper a lot when he was on the road, but in my version of this fairy tale, I had not expected to be sleeping in one. JR climbed up into the cab, closed the door, and said, "Well, let's get into the back and get comfortable, okay?"

"Okay," I said and climbed between the seats into the sleeper and laid down on the bunk rack it contained. For many people, including myself, a side- effect of weed is short-term memory loss. A lot of events can't be recalled or remembered, even a few minutes later, and sometimes events are pretty much a blur for a few hours. Often, the day after a good, long high very little can be remembered about what transpired during the time, you were high. That night, the weed was potent and honestly, a bit of luck for me. After JR started kissing me on the lips and rubbing my body all over, I became only vaguely aware of what was happening. Something felt somewhat nice for a little while, but after he had taken off my dress, bra, and panties, it was not the feeling I had anticipated; I was even luckier when I fell asleep soon after. When the early morning light came through the truck's windshield, I awoke not remembering much. I only knew I needed to use the bathroom and that I was sore down where my girl parts were.

The hopes that JR was my romantic Prince Charming and the happy life I would have being his wife disappeared the following day like a shimmering heat mirage on a summer highway at noon. He wasn't too concerned with my feelings or the fairy-tale fantasies I had when I got into the truck the first time. I rode with JR for a few long months stopping only those times to drop loads and pick up new ones, or spend a few days or so at an apartment JR had with some other truckers in Flagstaff, Arizona. The long nights I had to sleep in the uncomfortable sleeper with him were only slightly less tortuous than the days and nights at the apartment with him and his buddies. I diminished some of my dismay and painful body parts with as many liberal doses of alcohol and joints as I could get my hands on. There was so little difference between my role with JR and his buddies than my role at home. I was used and abused and received only a few tokens of appreciation with demands of more service to whatever their needs were at the moment. I was disgusted and felt completely betrayed within a month of walking out of the diner. Heartbroken by his lies and deceit, JR and his pals crushed my youthful romantic thinking by teasing me constantly as I poured drinks and served them food. I kept the apartment clean, doing everything they asked giving them whatever they wanted just hoping to be valued. I lost all belief in myself as my dignity and self-worth plummeted to zero. I learned the cold reality of men who are interested only in the denigration of women for their own pleasure. There are some good guys in the world, but I had not met them yet. I drank to drunkenness daily to deal with the humiliation as I continued to lose what little respect I had for myself. The safe place I had dreamed of with my first love wasn't going to be anywhere with JR, ever. When I could not take any more of the torture, I asked JR to return me home on his next trip back to Tombstone. He obliged me.

Knowing I was going to be completely beholden to Ma and that it would take the rest of my life to live it down, or most of it anyway, I dejectedly went to the house when JR dropped me off in Tombstone. It didn't start off well, and it never really got better. I was reminded daily by Ma of just how worthless I was, and I was a loser of a daughter that no one wanted. The fear and disgust of being home became unbearable and knowing the ugly reality of my future if I stayed in this small town was terrifying. I was looking to get out of Tombstone any way I could again just as soon as possible.

With little hope left for finding out who I wanted to be in this world or knowing how to make it happen, the reality of this place called "home" made it feel much less a home and more like a prison. On a Saturday afternoon down in the cellar, I was busy cleaning up and moving things around for Ma. As I was standing on a ladder taking down boxes that were stacked up to the ceiling, I grabbed a box and brought it down so Ma could go through it. Old toys from our childhood, pictures and documents, and clothing we had outgrown filled countless boxes. Ma said these things had been stored down here for years and were just collecting dust and taking up space.

Ma had gone upstairs while I was trying to get off the ladder with this huge box; I was not able to see below me and stepped down thinking I was on the last step but really was on the second step. I stepped off and felt my ACL snap, and fell to the floor in excruciating pain. My ACL had torn completely in half, and I could not move. Ma came back to the cellar asking, "What happened?" I was trying to explain while at the same time trying to stand up only to fall back to the floor. "Please Ma, take me to the hospital. I hurt my knee real bad," I said through my pain. We drove to the hospital, and after the X-rays were completed the doctor said it showed no broken bones but told Ma that I would need to see an orthopedic surgeon for a follow-up because an MRI was needed to know the real damage done, and then repair it.

I had NO Insurance, and Ma proclaimed quickly she was not going to pay for any more doctors. She said it was my own damn fault I fell, and I would have to take responsibility for my own stupidity. She repeated every morning for three days. If I needed anything else, Ma told me, I needed to 'do it for myself' for once. The words she spoke hurt me so badly, but the attitude was not really something new. It cut deep and made me feel small and helpless more so than I already did. How can I be so worthless, and why does anything I do cause her so much contempt? These were questions I had asked myself more often, and I never learned the answers nor how to dull the ache I felt.

All I could do was lay down or sit glumly with ice packs wrapped around my knee and a hospital knee brace from the crotch to my ankle strapped on to keep my leg straight and rigid. For three days, I endured frequent disparaging and petty remarks about my own carelessness being the cause of my injury. When the first few rebuttals I made to Ma about her accusations not being true, I was met with uglier remarks about the present being no different from a litany of long past and forgotten events. I decided it was better to just stay silent. Ma portrayed herself as a victim of my accident because she had to take time away from her normal activities to cook or help me get up and down to go to the bathroom or from couch to bed, however, she actually did little of either. Time had taught me that Ma would not give in to her promise of making me fend for myself. However, Ma didn't know that deep inside me was the hard-won emotional inner strength that I had developed in order to survive the life I lived under this roof.

I reached in to find it on the fourth day when I surrendered to my present reality. I found the courage to hobble down the stairs as I clenched my teeth and fought back any hint of a tear. Unsteady but not unsure, with arms raised up like little wings, I took the first few steps gingerly and began speaking softly and slowly words from a prayer written in my mind long, long, ago. "Yea thou I walk through the valley in the shadow of death, I shall fear no evil, for Thou art with me...." Psalms 23 became my prayer of courage, which I still repeat daily without fail.

I would not let the wall I put up that day against Ma's relentless emotional attacks ever be breached again. I would obey the voice in my head that whispered that day, "Forgive them for they are children," I did, and I will not ever forget those words.

When I could finally hobble around some, my mother was back to her demanding, slave driver self and would say to me, "I know you are just faking. Get up and do some chores." The hypocrisy of these words stung deeply because the injury happened while I was helping my mother and trying to be a good daughter. Nevertheless, Ma just could not stand me. About the same time as my accident, my precious little brother started having his own addiction issues undoubtedly due to Ma's unloving attitude and the brutal history Pa had imposed upon him. There would come a day that both Ma and myself would be forced to realize and accept just what the consequences were. Her aloofness and harsh critical demands would come back to haunt her. She would relentlessly deny that her parenting had any negative effects on my brother and me to avoid the shame and guilt others said was well deserved. It would be an awakening for her that would be too little, too late.

Why did I have such a sad life?

Why did I have to endure so much mental, emotional, and physical strife? Only God knows. Maybe, I guess to build character.

I had come to the realization that living in my parent's home was always going to be like living in prison. It was just walls and concrete, no warmth, no love, and definitely not a home. The ugly words, nearly constant as long as I could remember, the fights, the bruises, all of it Satan working his tricks trying to make me feel shameful as if it was my fault. I accepted that I was the only one I could count on to find my way, so I began my prayers every night for God to show me the direction to a better life. I was physically fit and healthy before the fall, now I willed myself daily to overcome the physical injuries and restore my heart and mind. I wanted to walk without crutches or a cane, and finding a job soon was my top priority because I was going to start over. I borrowed Ma's car to try to find work in town one day and wondered, "Do I stay here and deal with life as it is or find a better way of life far from here?" I had only been home a few days when I tore my ACL and had not paid much attention to the fact I had missed my period. When I realized I was pregnant, I was scared and wondered what I was going to do, so I told my Ma the facts.

I was told to get an abortion or leave home. With no money and no way to get anywhere, I felt alone and helpless, so I complied with Ma's demands. Giving up the baby was hard, but I knew it was for the best since I had no way to take care of myself let alone a newborn infant. I had taken a couple of weeks to heal before I went searching for a job again and either luck or God, or both, was on my side. I found an opportunity at the truck stop near the main interstate where they needed a waitress, and I definitely needed a job. Working in restaurants for almost four years by now, I was sure I could do it. I went in to talk with the manager early one morning. We sat down, and I began by telling him, "I've never regularly waitressed before, but I used to help out at the diner in town serving customers when they would get busy and were shorthanded. Please give me a chance, and I'll prove myself to you. I learn quickly, and I'll work really hard." I gave the manager a big smile and waited for his answer.

I reminded myself that waitressing was a job skill I could take with me anywhere, including that magical place far from here once I had the money.

That new destination in mind was; **Happiness, Anywhere – USA.**

I looked imploringly at the manager and felt anxious as I waited for him to decide if I was worth taking the chance on. Finally, he says, "Okay you can start Friday." "Thanks. You will not be sorry. I will fit right in here," I told him with another big smile. I was working again and the future just got a little brighter. He paired me with Peggy, the head server, and I followed her lead for a few days to learn how the system in the truck stop worked. Picking up the routine quickly, I felt confident I was ready to work the floor on my own. Peggy was grateful for my initiative because she had been shorthanded for weeks now and was tired of running the place virtually alone. The manager, Tim, gave me a small station in the back of the place and told me if I needed any help to let him know. Now that I was able to make some money, and save, I set my plan into action to get as far away from Tombstone, Texas as fast as I possibly could.

Peggy liked me and told me the trick was to get the customers to like you quickly and give them what they wanted with a smile. I had figured that out long ago, though I just smiled at Peggy and said, "Okay." Using my cute little smile and talking with my customers, I was making good money very quickly. The restaurant was busy with long-haul truckers who flirted with me, and I used it to my advantage. I was told often just how 'cute' I was; they loved looking at my pretty, little, freckled face, and I returned their kindness with beaming smiles and thanked them knowing what they really were looking at as I walked away.

Peace and happiness were awaiting me just down the road somewhere, and I was determined to find it, wherever it might be. I prayed daily and prayed for my little one in heaven, too. God was still nearby even on those sad days and events that just seemed to keep coming at me, and when the uncertainty filled me, along with days when I felt I was losing my faith. I still held fast to my dreams, trusting I would be alright if only I could just get through the day. "One day at a time" was my new mantra. Sometimes I felt that all my accomplishments were pointless, and it was like they never happened as my Ma continued to beat me down emotionally. Except, the Lord was on my side and wasn't going to be defeated that easily. He pushed me along steadily.

The dreams and desire were to find someone to love, get married, have babies, and take care of a family – isn't that what life is all about? I believed it true, and my hope was strong that it was going to happen and be my path to happiness. My Aunt Janna had told me one day when she had stopped in the restaurant where I now worked that, "None of the folks in your family seemed happy," and "Don't be like your Ma and Pa," as they were the dysfunctional role models I had to follow. I told my aunt that I would do my best to be happy, wished her a great day, and thanked her. Not knowing much about life outside of this town and being stuck in a place that had limited opportunities and violence, I needed to be able to talk to someone. My late Grammy and Aunt Janna were the only ones who I could really talk to, but I thought that Aunt Hazel could help too. So, I stopped by her house on a cool evening just before sunset.

I asked my Auntie, "Why does my Ma treat me so bad? She's always telling me I'm worthless, that she wishes I never was born," Aunt Hazel was Ma's sister, and if anyone could help me it was her. She looked at me with tears in her eyes and said, "Tiffy, I don't know what to tell you except that's just the way she is." I looked at her wondering if she knew if it was just me Ma didn't love or was she like that with everyone. Does Ma care for my little brother at all, and if so, why does he seem as messed up emotionally as I am? We talked awhile over some warm tea, and I left feeling grateful to have Aunt Hazel in my life. Knowing Aunt Hazel thought I was still special was one reason I could keep going in life.

I had worked a very long shift one night and was sitting lazily on the front porch trying to enjoy the early morning sounds of the birds singing and watching as the world came to life. With my leg propped up and an ice pack on my knee, I was hoping to get the swelling down and the throbbing pain to recede. Thinking maybe Aunt Hazel could help with some other questions I had, I decided I would go over there later and tell her just how bad I was hurting inside, hoping she could tell me what I should do. I didn't hear my Pa step out onto the porch, so I was startled by his harsh voice.

"Girl what are you doing out here? Get in there, and do your chores," he barked. I was constantly listening to Ma telling me to do this, that, or the other, all while knowing my knee was not healed which caused me great difficulty. I was living in constant physical pain now and doing the best I could to walk and work, not to mention constantly being reminded of just how useless I was by my Ma. I was fed up after all I had done for them without receiving an ounce of gratitude or love. Nothing I would ever do could change their attitudes; without mercy, they only felt anger and resentment towards me. I had tried everything I could think of to make my Ma and Pa proud of me, for them to feel happy and be proud that I was their daughter. I was so tired of being a slave, and that is really all it boiled down to. I yelled back at Pa, "NO! I won't do anymore." It was time for me to stand up for myself, and the time was now.

As Pa raised his hand to hit me, I looked him right in the eyes daring him to do it. I had definitely grown up a bit since the last time he hit me. His face went red and then a little slack, and I knew he was startled by a defiant look of power he had never seen in me before; even I was sensing a force inside me rising to confront an evil-natured man who would regret his latest, unjustified malice forever. He had pushed and pummeled me too many times, and I was determined that it would not happen again, at least not without a fight. Maybe it was a wounded animal instinct drawn up from deep within for self-preservation, or maybe it was something else, something left behind from a child's inability to confront an adult on his own terms. Either way, acceptance of the immediate reality shifted my position and choice from fear and weakness to courage and power. A flickering light in my soul illuminated briefly showing me the way straight ahead.

Pa held his swing and said; "Get out! You need to leave, now!" I stood up calmly, went inside, and quickly packed what I could carry. I went through the front door knowing I had a better life ahead and should have never come back here in the first place. It was never home. Stopping by Auntie Hazel's house on my way to the bus station for an encouraging word and warm hug, I let her know how grateful I was for all she had done for me over the years, especially since Grammy passed, and I said goodbye.

 Tears filled both of our eyes as I said, goodbye, to Texas.

With strength and courage sufficient to meet my needs, I boarded the Greyhound bus in hopes of happiness, love, and freedom from all the abuse life had brought me. Trusting I had made the right choice with such an unknown future, and counting, once again, the few dollars I had saved, I was glad I had bought the ticket to carry me away to sunny south Florida.

In the mid-eighties, Fort Lauderdale was 'The Place' for spring break and retirees; it was a waitress' gold mine. Well, it was if you were any good at it. High school and college kids came there to party and celebrate their lives coming into adulthood, a place where they believed they had control over what they did and how they did it. Young adults getting drunk and high at wild hotel parties, staggering out to the pool or beach to party, sexing any willing partner, not realizing the potential lifestyle hazards they were setting themselves up for in their future. The retirees flocked there from the north, too, during the cold, winter months to enjoy the warm weather at the beach by day and casual, leisurely lifestyle by night. With all of these people filling the hotels and restaurants, the potential to make money with my new skills appeared near endless. I was on my way there, right now, to find out for myself.

I feared for my brother I had left behind but, there was no way for me to protect him and myself any longer. Mikey was going to have to find his own strength, and hopefully his way out of Ma's house and the abuse because I was forced to protect only myself now. With the hope of peace on the horizon, I boarded that bus heading east trembling a little but trying not to let my fear and anxiety show. I was a teenager heading across the USA alone, and I had never been more scared yet more certain at the same time. I took my seat on the bus, closed my eyes, and said the first of many prayers I hoped God was hearing.

The week was long, as I stared out the window as we rolled along, and then stopped every couple of hours through the day and night, into and out of the big cities and tiny towns along the route. The low, steady hum of the bus's engine lulled me in and out of little naps and quiet time reflecting on what I left behind and what might be ahead. It gave me the time I needed to come to terms with my decision and why I had made it when I did. The scenery steadily changed outside my window, as did the people on the bus. The brown, brushy plains of Texas gave way to the lush greenery of south Louisiana marshlands. We crossed the big, wide Mississippi river, and I felt alive and more positive and hopeful of what lay ahead of me. As we drove into New Orleans, I initially thought it might be a good place to get off the bus and stay, but as I sat in the bus depot waiting for the bus driver to refuel, it just did not feel right to me as my original plan. So, I re-boarded, and we continued east along Interstate I-10, passing through Alabama and into Florida; I was growing more excited as the miles passed.

Thoughts of what was waiting for me out there on the horizon kept me smiling in anticipation as day turned to night, and I drifted off to sleep thinking about the beautiful, blue ocean I would soon swim in. I saw myself lying on the white, sandy beaches under a warm sun with the sound of happy people all around me relaxing and enjoying a life I had wanted for so long.

I woke the next morning to a smiling face. A girl named Sara, who had boarded the bus in New Orleans and taken the seat across the aisle from me, was already awake and anxiously awaiting the day ahead. I reached in my backpack and pulled out a bottle of water when I noticed she was watching me intently. Smiling at her, I asked if she would like a bottle, also, and handed one to her before she could answer. We both were young and nervous. We started talking about why we were on the bus heading east, and she said, "I am going home to get away from a bad relationship." I told Sara about JR and my bad experience, too, and wished her much happiness when she got back home. I really was a good girl with a big heart, and I could definitely relate to her. I always wanted the best for others, and sharing our stories lessened our anxieties as the miles rolled on, both of us talking about fresh starts and the courage it took to start over. Two brave, young ladies, praying for a better life, forged a bond of kinship amid the search and struggle of finding their way and a better life ahead. When the bus stopped in Tallahassee, we said our goodbyes, wished each other the best, and we moved on into the unknowns of the journey ahead.

I felt it had been quite the adventure so far, and I was proud of myself that I had made the trip. I arrived after another long night, in sunny Ft Lauderdale, just as the sun was coming up. I walked out of the bus terminal into the bright sunlight alone, in a strange place, with only the little bit of money I had saved, feeling only a little apprehensive. The long ride and Sara's company had given me time to sort out some things about myself as far as what I was capable of and how I might achieve my dream. I found a pay-by-the-week motel a half-hour walk from the ocean, settled in, and started planning my next steps. It was a sunny day with the warm southern breeze blowing off the ocean, and I felt this was going to be a good place to start over. Aunt Hazel had driven me to the bus station in the next town over from Tombstone and bought me a calling card on the way there. She asked me to please give her a call and let her know when I got to Florida safely. I found a payphone and made the call, telling my Aunt all about Sara and all the cool things I had seen so far. She was glad to hear from me and told me to be safe, pay attention to things around me, and wished me well. I promised I would call as often as possible.

Deciding that I would take a day to enjoy my new surroundings, I headed out to the beach for a swim and some sun. I had a good feeling and felt sure about the choice I had made so far; I made a leap of utter faith with near-infinite courage, and I guess you could say it was a happy landing. Lying out in the sun watching the other beach-goers building sandcastles with their kids and laughing, I was saddened that I had no memories of anything closely related to this kind of family fun. A calm fell over me as I listened to the sound of the waves as they rolled onshore, filling my soul with peace, and I was hoping this would be a sign of things to come in my new life. Filled with a simple serenity from my quiet day, I picked up my towel and headed to the small showers up by the sidewalk, rinsed off the sand, and headed back to my room to change. There was block after block of hotels facing the ocean, bars and clubs lining the streets, high-end restaurants ready and waiting to serve all the traveling folks enjoying the South Florida hot spot. It had to be Paradise.

I decided to take a leisurely walk on the Strip. As I was walking I saw drunken boys pulling at vulnerable, intoxicated girls unable to defend themselves, and the anger arose in me knowing I could not watch this daily. I witnessed a staggering girl being dragged away by her boyfriend and overheard him yell, "You will do him if I tell you!" I quickly realized I was actually looking at a local hooker and her pimp. Disgust simmered in me at the thought of how anyone could allow himself or herself to be in that position; I felt morally outraged and vowed to myself I would never get so low that I would have to sell my body, for money. I watched as the pimp slammed the door to the hotel room closed; I felt bad for the girl, and I figured she was going to get beat.

All I ever wanted was happiness and peace, things I only briefly ever felt in my life. An incredibly brave, small-town girl was now on the other side of the country, alone, and looking for a place to rest without fear, yelling, or brutality; I was very proud of myself for taking the risk. I discovered quickly all the rum I had started drinking again was causing serious problems. So, I stopped drinking, and after a few days without it, I could feel the difference in my body. That dull ache in my liver had subsided, and that soft whisper that kept pushing me forward was speaking to me again, or maybe I was just beginning to hear it again.

I set out early one morning to go job hunting in the area close by and discovered there was plenty to choose from. I found a job easily within a few hours the first day, praise God. I began waitressing at a popular seafood restaurant, The Lobster Shanty, where the customers could choose their own live lobster, watch it pulled from the tank, and then later, have it cracked open tableside. From the first day, I was making good money because I knew the right routines by heart. Serving drinks and fresh lobster with a big Texas smile and a willing demeanor to go the extra mile to earn a good tip, I was finding that things were getting better every day, and within a few weeks, I thought to myself, "I did it!" The pride and self-esteem I thought I'd lost now were starting to rise again, and a glimmer of real happiness was showing through. The despondent, quiet girl that arrived in Florida just a dozen weeks ago was quietly disappearing.

After a couple of months of hard work, I was able to afford a small, one-bedroom apartment, and not too much longer after that a used car to drive. Sweet success! I was not going to miss that stinky bus, but riding it every day enabled me to save every penny I could, and I worked my best charm to earn the tips I needed to raise myself to the next level. I bought a few used glasses and dishes, along with some new dresses and shoes from the local Goodwill, and I felt life was steadily building into something good.

I had fun at work with the other servers, and Amy, who had been my trainer, was now becoming a close friend. Amy and I started getting together outside of work. We enjoyed shopping or going to the beach laying out in the sun, watching the boys try to surf in the shallow waves, and just being successful young singles. This new life and the simple things that gave me so much peace was all I could have ever hoped for; I had worked smart and steady for what I had achieved, and I was extremely thankful for it. I was rebuilding my torn-apart, emotional life, and I was thriving. I was carrying myself with new hard-earned self-respect inside that felt good, and the people around me let me know it was showing on the outside, as well.

Amy was also a transplant from up north somewhere; she told me she didn't miss it and was happy being in the warm Florida weather. One night after work, we decided to meet up at a bar down on the boardwalk. I walked into the club and heard music blaring and saw everyone having a good time dancing; good-looking guys were everywhere. Amy was already at the bar waiting so I went over and sat down next to her saying, "I see a cute guy over there looking at you; maybe he'll come over here if you give him a little smile." We both laughed, and I smiled at the boy across the room, he smiled back, pulled away from the table, and headed our way. "Oh my God, Amy, here he comes!" I blurted out.

A knot formed in my belly immediately as he walked towards us because, until now, I had not really thought about having a boyfriend again. Amy had already had a couple of drinks before I arrived, and I had belted down a couple to calm myself before I left my apartment after not drinking at all for a couple of weeks. As the cute guy approaches us, we both look at each other and giggled with that female awareness of what we had just started. He stopped and stood beside our table, a little overconfident because of the liquor he had consumed, and with a self-assured voice said, "Hey girls! Wow, you're both so cute! Do you want to dance?" Amy said, "Sure, I'd love to!" and smiled at him. I declined to make it a threesome on the dance floor and felt the knot in my stomach tighten just a bit. "I'm Jared by the way," he smiled at me then took Amy out on the dance floor. They danced a few songs before returning to our table excited, hot, and sweaty from the intensity of the fast music and alcohol. The three of us hung out most of the night, talking, teasing, and drinking. I did not realize the resident evil lurking in Jared that first night and unwittingly, I allowed it into my life again. We continued talking and dancing, we told him about the restaurant we worked at, asking him what kind of work he did, and where he was from. "I'm in the construction industry; my specialty is irrigation." He stated proudly.

Amy, already bored by him, got up from the table and told me she would see me tomorrow at work and left. Jared and I had another drink, listened to some more music, and talked. He escorted me to my car politely at closing time. Jared made me promise that he could see me again soon. Commenting on the stars above and telling me I was just as beautiful, I let my guard down just a little. I said, "Sure, I would like that a lot," and thanked him for the compliment with a shy blushing smile before giving him my phone number. Intoxicated and a little starry-eyed by his charming wit, I felt happy because he seemed so nice and I was excited at the thought of Mr. Right finally coming my way. I did not know he came with habits and heavy emotional baggage, and it would remain hidden for the length of time it took me to trust him and fall in love with his charm and the way he made me feel safe and secure. He would later introduce me to the powerful and persuasive evil power of the shiny 'White Fire' that would steal my very soul.

A very fortunate thing happened one evening at the restaurant during the off-season when business was slow, and I had more time to give to my customers. A very nice couple I recognized as regulars had been seated at one of my tables and ordered up a bottle of white wine and a couple of lobsters from the tank. I had just brought them their salads when the gentleman introduced himself and his wife to me and asked me if I ever thought about going back to school.

Mr. Jones told me that this was the boom of the personal computer. It was 1982, and IBM was introducing the PC to the public for private use. I stood there for a moment looking around the restaurant to see if anyone new had been seated before I acknowledged my interest in what he was saying. With an inquisitive glance at his wife and her nodded approval, I answered, "Well, sometimes I think about it." Mr. Don Jones smiled and began to share what was on his mind.

"They are going to need lots of technicians to build these computers, along with repairing them, and giving support to the public."

I listened intently as Mr. Jones explained to me all about how the world was going to change, and I could be part of its growth. He shared with me how corporations using monster-sized systems that networked internally within the buildings, would now be able to network globally using smaller-sized systems. He told me this technology was for the public, too, and not just for big corporations anymore. I said, "Wow that's awesome, but I have no idea how to get signed up for school or where I would even get the money."

I loved to learn and I was intrigued by what he was saying, so I listened intently while watching the activity of customers coming and going. Mr. Jones told me about a startup technology school in Davie, Florida that was helping students get government grants to fund their education. After what seemed like hours of on and off exchanges between him and me while they finished their dinner and I served other customers, I thanked him and his wife profusely for taking the time to share his knowledge with me.

As I had promised him, I was down there the next day inquiring about what I needed to do, to qualify. It was just as Mr. Jones had said, Electronics was and is the future, so I enrolled knowing it was a chance to compete and excel which I thrived on.

I was excited for the chance to be a part of a growing industry and the technology that would soon change the world. The small tech school, known then as Keiser Technology Institute, had become a fully accredited University twenty-five years later. They helped me get that government funding grant, and I was off to learn. Being the only girl in the class posed some problems, mostly within myself. I was still just a bit shy, but I ignored most of the ugly looks or whispers as to why I was in the class.

The training was intense as I learned about current flow, what resistors, capacitors, and memory chips all did, and more importantly why. We learned the value of respecting the voltage, and I even tested it by accident on occasion. Mr. Hess was a good teacher and was always willing to stay late and help any of us to make sure we succeeded in our training. I was in the first class to graduate from Keiser, so I imagine he had a lot riding on us. Absorbing all there was to learn about this new technology, the small components inside the circuit panels, understanding what each part was tasked to do, the testing procedures to trace the circuit paths depending on the function needed, was intense and thorough.

5

SHINING BRIGHT!

I really did not care about what those boys thought or said because I was there to learn and nothing else. The determination and dedication it took for me to succeed increased daily as I excelled even beyond my own expectations. Working forty hours a week at night and attending school forty hours a week by day was challenging indeed.

SUCCESS! go get it...

I graduated with top honors and at the top of the class with a

3.98 GPA. With my Associate's Degree, the future was now mine for the taking and a career that would soon follow. I worked very hard for my success, to be happy, and to have all those things in life that society says we should have. I also worked hard to build a personal life; the friends I had at work gave me inspiration, and I had a lot to smile about, but it was time to find a new job. A job where I could put my newly learned skills to work, and I located a company in Boca Raton that had just opened up, building custom PC computers for individuals and small companies.

It was a great honor for this twenty-year-old girl to undertake by being the only female on the assembly floor. I picked up my new trade with purpose and humility. I forced myself to continue retraining or learning to improve my skill set in order to feel better about myself, and to show the men around me that I could work just as hard as they did. George, another tech working closely with me, struggled on many days after putting his systems together, building them to spec, testing them, and then packaging the computers for shipping. I would encourage him and helped him when no one else was around. Apparently, it did not go unnoticed by the bosses as eight months later they promoted me to assembly floor supervisor due to growing QC issues I rapidly resolved.

Over the next two years, I worked my way up from assembler, to QC testing tech, then manager of the production floor. I had accepted Mr. Jones' guidance, and I was very proud of what I had accomplished. I had overcome so many obstacles and barriers in my short life, and all my prayers were answered by faith and self-discipline. I finally saw a secure, self-made, happy, pretty girl in the mirror that once reflected shame and self-doubt. I had glimpsed, for a few precious moments, my reflection of peace and hope unbounded. I had reached that place we all strive to find and share with others in our lives. My future never seemed better or more fulfilled. I was shining brighter on the inside than the happy smile I wore on the outside allowed me.

I had succeeded beyond my own expectations and participated in the birth of a revolution in technology. I was there at the very beginning with my hands on the wheel into the new age of electronics. I was praised often by peers, women and men alike, and awarded multiple times for my instrumental part in this new industry. Wow, thirty-plus years later it is incredible to see where the industry has developed. Mr. Jones had no idea just how important or sought after the PC would become or how the industries would expand to cell phones that fit in your back pocket while having the power of a room-sized mainframe computer inside it. The palm pilot, which was the first handheld minicomputer, now a tablet, TV's and monitors that weighed so much that 2 people were needed to carry them, and now lightweight monitors that can easily be mounted to a wall. My personal success reduced my dependency on drugs and alcohol to near zero. After almost two years of freedom from substances, Jared chained Tiffany Rose Baker in Hell, and I became a functioning addict in an upwardly mobile career. I was doing really well when I was caught in the subtle, persuasive trap of a white fire called Cocaine. Jared coaxed me into trying it a few short months after we had met. My early, staunch refusals gave way to his charm and insistence that it was 'okay' to sniff up the tiny lines of cocaine from the mirror. They would make me feel really good; just try it once, please, he insisted. The fateful words, 'If you love me,' said over and over again, finally wore me down, and I betrayed my hard-fought sobriety of putting down the bottle and the joint. The occasional weekend tries at first. Jared would bring about in me a desire for all of the wrong material things and terrible lifestyle choices.

   I would slowly betray the true source of my gifts, The Lord, my Higher Power.
   All too soon, it became apparent the popular, hard-working, Texas Belle was mortally wounded by something.

   During this time, they transferred me to the office area while I was pregnant, so I was able to learn the business side of the company. I was still focused and disciplined while working on data entry and other office functions for Gulfstream. These secretarial skills proved to be valuable in my future. Although I had been successful, the birth of my daughter Crystal and my increasing cocaine use would soon force me to resign from my position at Gulfstream Computers.

I knew God was there somewhere, and the soft whisper I heard now and again assured me of it, but I was taking for granted the gifts given, and I did not consider the fact that I could lose them, as easily as I received them. My fatal mistake was allowing my successes to give me a false sense of bravado that caused me to only trust in myself, my possessions, and it was not going to end well.

Before Jared, I was reasonably cautious and conservative in all I did, and with good reasons. I had learned tough lessons from Pete, JR, and others and remembered them well. Let's flashback to when I first met Jared at the club.

I had purposely limited the amount of time I spent off-task in my work and school. His charm took me by surprise though, and I enjoyed his exciting and adventurous nature. He was a young man trying to prove to me that he was a good provider, and his arrogant, yet hard-working personality made me smile, again, about love's potential. Yet, I totally missed God trying to warn me about the future if I stayed with Jared. The unfortunate truth was that I was hearing God, but I was not listening to anything other than the exciting new beating of my heart. I became blinded by the worldly knowledge and materials things Jared brought to my life.

At first, he was so sweet by taking me out to fancy restaurants to have prime rib dinners and drinks, walking the beach at night holding hands, watching the stars in the sky quietly hanging there above the darkness of the ocean as it rolled softly onshore. I believed I was really in love. The sex so intense and comfortable in the beginning, and I thought I had found my true love, but Jared subtlety brought the evils of his world into mine with smooth, cunning deception. Upon his first betrayal, the past began repeating itself.

I felt a sense of belonging the day we moved into the new house we bought, something I had only ever hoped to feel, and it was deeply fulfilling. I was happily unpacking dishes in my own, new kitchen at twenty-five when Jared walks in and dumps an 8-ball of cocaine on a plate, and hands me a straw. "Here baby, have a hit and we will knock this unpacking out in no time." I look up at him, from the line of coke he just laid out for me, stuck the straw in my nose, inhaled deeply, and immediately I could feel my heart racing. I gave him a kiss, wiped the coke from around my nose, and continued with what I was doing. Before the night was over, the plate was empty, and all the boxes were unpacked. The next afternoon, as I was waiting impatiently for Jared to get home and bring more drugs, I felt anxious and frustrated. I had that sense women get when there is another woman in the picture, and you just do not know it yet. Jared had stopped at the bar, he said, when he finally arrived home. He handed me a bag of coke; I took it, cut out a line, and all too soon forgot about his latest betrayal. Sadly, this became an all too common event for Jared and me as both of our addictions began to unfold in live time. I had been led into a wicked world unknowingly while holding the hand of a man I trusted. I had never known or cared to know of cocaine, let alone use it, and now I was addicted. He had let me down, and I knew it. It hurt, but I tried to keep the truth from my mind, and more so my heart, hoping somehow I could fix it.

Although I was proud of myself at work, I was very insecure about my relationship with Jared which aided him in blinding me to walk the road I was now walking. The cruel basis of my weakness was that precious thing Pete had stolen from me, and it mercilessly grew a garden of self-doubts about my womanhood. Just before I had gotten pregnant, I learned Jared was cheating on me. Jared, even more than an alcoholic or drug addict, was a sex addict. Yes, there is such a thing. There was no amount of depravity that he wouldn't participate in, and this is a foretelling of the evil darkness I would be thrown into. A place of disgrace and shame, a place I thought I had escaped from by leaving Texas. This man whom I thought would help me and love me so I could be the woman I was always hoping to be – a mother, wife, and best friend – plunged me down into disgrace without any shame or mercy. He only wanted to degrade me and use me, and he did so by keeping me high. Ultimately, he needed to destroy my self-worth in order to make me dependent on him without alternatives.

The past started to repeat itself and it would prove to either help me see that I needed to escape or stay trapped and wither away while absorbing more abuse emotionally, more so, than physically. This second significant relationship in life usually becomes the husband or wife, and so it was with me. This was a case of dominance and abusive control over the submissive partner while using drugs as the controlling method; it is a vicious cycle.

> I was now *trapped* and felt nothing anymore!

With the happiness of a good life that I had built for myself escaping by the minute, I began a slow death spiral down into an emotional and physical hell. I desperately tried to hold on to the little bit of happiness I had, but I was crying myself to sleep, that is when I could sleep at all. Everything I had worked so hard to achieve – the self-respect, self-worth, self-preservation, and survival skills – were going up in smoke, up my nose really, and it was choking the very life from me.

I just wanted to escape from the ugly reality all around me. I realized that Pete, JR, and all their pals were only after one thing. It's not a cliche. Most men, though not all men are just dogs in heat. I believe males innately believe that they have the right to treat women as nothing more than a possession for their entertainment and sexual satisfaction.

Although I was saddened by the circumstances with Jared, I could not get enough coke up my nose to dull the emotional torment and escape the reality I existed in. I had also found out more than three years after meeting Jared and plunging into this drug-induced feast that I was pregnant with our second child. Jared had worked very hard and supported our addiction with a certain level of prestige. He would stay high all night and work all day; it seemed to be all life had to offer for him. He was a perfect example of the hypocrisy of addiction and that which leads most people to a fatal end. We believe we can function in society, care for our households, and enjoy, in abundance, that which holds us, prisoner. We believe we are not addicts, and that is dead wrong – pun intended! I was just too insecure to see the truth and much too broken inside to fight. Ironically, fighting was all we ever seemed to do, as our loud voices echoed off the walls any time I kept my clothes on and we were together.

"What kind of man do you want, Tiffany? Some rich guy that has time to take you everywhere and do everything to make you feel like you really are somebody? Is that what you want? Would that make you happy," Jared screamed. "No," I respond bursting into tears.

Jared continued his rant without a pause. "Well, you sure got me fooled. Nobody forced the coke up your nose. You are the one who is being so arrogant now. You used to want to screw all the time, and now you hardly ever want to at all. I finally found somebody who wants to make me happy, and now you are all high and mighty about it. I love you, and you know that, but I need more than just a once-a-week quickie with you. You cannot just suddenly cut me off and claim that I am some pervert whorehound just because you don't want to do a threesome. How do I know that you didn't do it with somebody else long before I met you? You sure seemed the type. Who else got you high and screwed you before I came along? Who Tiffy? How many times?"

"Please, Jared, stop. I am pregnant again, and you do not even care! I cannot keep doing the crazy shit you want to do all the time. I cannot just go on thinking that it's okay anymore. I do not sleep, I do not eat enough, and it makes me sick to think about what is happening to the baby. I don't want to kill our baby; don't you understand?" I pleaded with tears in my eyes and God-fearing desperation in my soul. Even though I was pregnant, I could not stop using. I knew I was putting my baby at risk and hated myself for it. All I could do was pray that God would protect my child growing inside of me. God must have heard me too, because even after snorting an 8-ball a day, I was finally able to eat right, exercise, and sleep. Yes, that is almost impossible under the circumstances of what I was using; it was definitely not the norm. Sadly, Jared had little concern for his unborn child and never once tried to get me to stop using while I carried his babies. When Johnnie was born in 1990, I prayed for days before his birth that I would not lose him to the system, but it still didn't deter me from using it. Crystal was born in 1987 during a time when the hospitals were not testing infants for drugs, especially with parents that seemed to be so successful. Both of our kids were cocaine babies.

God had heard my prayers, and my little baby boy was healthy by His grace.

I was still psychologically overwhelmed by my addiction sickness, and it continued soon after I got home. I was too frightened by Jared and the possible consequences if I told anybody the truth about my addiction, so I was stuck between a rock and a hard place, so to speak, and didn't get the help I needed. Fear was a powerful force to maintain my submission and helplessness. Jared used it to the maximum advantage to maintain his control over me and safeguard his evil obsessions and power.

Jared knew I was positively hooked and began withholding my drugs to get compliance with his sexual depravity. I hated him and all that he forced on me. I withdrew further as I became completely and utterly disgusted by Jared and the perversion of what he still wanted even now that he was a daddy; I felt tortured beyond my capacity to handle it all. My sheer survival of the nightmarish events required numbing myself to a zombie-like state so as to perform the circus animal requests, but I also had to have a level of clear-headedness in order to care for my children. It was only a matter of time before the inevitable would finally happen. I held on, with desperation to my oft-repeated prayers; Please God, spare my children from destruction.

In those strange surreal clear moments or perhaps I hallucinated, that I spent with God; I wished I had listened to those people that God had sent along the way to help me. The encouraging words by those few like Aunt Hazel, who told me just how strong I was and reminded me of just how far I had come and all the tragedy I overcame. How I wished I had spoken up to the school nurse, or maybe even a teacher, and shared my silent suffering. I felt horrible shame and isolation for all that I had done; I could not be forced to believe God would even want to bring me back from hell that I had descended upon willingly. All I could do was cry myself to sleep most nights in horrible fear of Him for what I had done. Lost inside and trying to make sense of how my family was already so torn apart by me, I began the worst detachment from reality when I believed I had committed an unforgivable sin and would suffer in Hell, or even die for it. Defeated emotionally in every way, getting high was all I could do to avoid insidious thoughts of suicide. I had no strength or willpower left due to the slow, torturous descent that brought me down into eternal darkness.

How could this be?

Jared was supposed to have protected me, loved me, his daughter, and now our son. All he cared about was getting drunk, high, and sexing anyone he could while I hopelessly retreated into that dark unforgivable place inside myself, the place I had once pulled myself out of years ago. How could I end all the tragedy Jared was causing and the very ugly forces he thrust in motion and imposed with absolute tyranny?

I heard the same words as I did when I was a little girl listening to my parents screaming in the dark, "It's all your fault!" What effect will it have on my own daughter or son lying in their beds in the dark at night listening to those same words as I did? What fear is running through their little souls while Jared forces the insatiable, ugly, animal acts upon me while being lost in another world of evil intoxication? I can't end my own life and leave them alone with him or in this world. I couldn't. I wouldn't.

Maybe little Crystal was also pondering the life she had found herself in as she laid in the bed listening to her parents just as I had those many years ago. Was she frightened? I checked on my children often, although high out of my mind and not liking myself very much, but too weak to stop it. I didn't stop loving her or my new little boy ever. The drug feast continued daily with neither of their parents obviously caring for anything other than and others might believe, their own selfish need to get high.

She had no idea what she was born into. Would she end up in the same drug-induced escapism as her parents? Could there be a way to break the cycle of Generational Dysfunction and the power of drugs that are so often its cause? Can a family that has only ever known it as just 'normal family stuff' ever escape at all? Would I ever find the strength to make that happen and save my children from reliving my life of torment and destruction?

My love of cocaine and drug suppressed morality couldn't overcome the forces that were denying me the power I needed to prevent the destruction of all I loved and valued.

Jared too had come from pretty much the same alcoholic world as I, though his father did much worse than just beat the crap out of him. Jared had also run from home to escape the abuse and turned into the same thing he came from, and I was just as void now as my mother was back then. Yes, I had accepted that in this current state of mind, I did a lousy job protecting my children. Thank God the Lord was still there, even when I didn't feel worthy of Him. Because of His unconditional love, he protected my children and me.

Did my daily, faithful, truthful prayers touch God's heart? There is no other answer.

"Follow me"

Trust that you can do this and find a better way, he whispers to my soul.

Yes, the Lord was still present in my life, but I was not hearing His voice or recognizing the gifts and blessings He sufficiently placed in my path. My mental faculties were seriously impaired, and I was in denial. Maybe if I had listened to the counselor at rehab, or was it a mental hospital staffer, who one day was trying to tell me that my addiction was only going to *get worse* from here, if I did not stop using now, my adventure through the Devil's funhouse would have ended much sooner.

Therefore, if you recognize any of what you have read so far in your life or others, please listen to me; if, with what you have read, you think it is bad at this point for me, or for you or them, heed my warning, and get help or get them help. If you don't, well, keep reading because you have not even gotten to the worst of it yet. Trust me. Maybe it will save your life or someone's life you love. Trust that you can overcome this terrible life of addiction and find a better way. Jared and his friend, Bob, had formed their own sprinkler business, and the money flowed in and right up all our noses. The late '80s and early '90s were a time of huge growth for South Florida. Condominiums, housing communities, and shopping plazas were going up everywhere; for so many years there was more work than time to get it all done. Great, you would think, except Jared was a drunken pervert with too much money in his hands. He had the power to control me with the money he made and bought the drugs he needed to enforce his will on me, and all the while I believed there was no safe way out. I was so addicted I put up with all of it just to stay high. With all the cheating, lies, and abuse Jared showed no concern about his psychopathic need for any and all kinds of things sexual, and I was glad when I wouldn't have to deal with it anymore. I learned too late he had been using the street girls since the beginning of our relationship, and now he turned almost completely to them to satisfy his obsession for illicit sex I wouldn't perform.

From here, the story goes from really ugly to grotesque; Jared would bring hookers home to sex him. Still hoping I would join in on the reindeer games as we all got high, so he continued to ask. This just completely sickened me, and I focused on what I could do to protect Crystal and Johnnie from what was happening around them. Though still too weak to pick up and leave so soon after a recent mental hospital and rehab stint, I just couldn't get a grip on life, or maybe I just didn't want to anymore. Seriously, how could things be this bad? I asked myself this question daily as my addiction spun out of control.

Jared was always eager for a party and put into action all of the kinky stuff he had floating around in his head; he was ready to make his dreams a reality at a moment's notice. Even knowing how bad I had screwed up my life, I was now forced to live in his fast lane, and I couldn't get high and zombie out fast enough. There was no such word as "enough" in his book and eventually mine, as everything was falling apart, and I felt powerless to stop it. The substantial sums of money Jared was earning created for us an illusion that we were invincible; we had it all. We were successful and cursed at the same time. In the beginning, it was a good life that we were driving after, but somewhere along the way, we ended up in a ditch. The grim truth was well on its way like a runaway freight train in the night with us tied on the tracks.

By this point, Jared was no longer able to drive at night. He could drive during the day because the courts allowed him to get a work permit which forced him to stop at the bar for his girl toys, and a pocket full of drugs to go along with them, on his way home from work. I spent many nights getting high, and then driving Jared's latest sex find back to the streets. One night, just before the sun came up I had to drive a girl, Lisa, back to the streets. She was Jared's newest find from the night before, and he had picked her up on his way home from the bar after work. It was a week or so before his second DUI, and the last time he would bring anyone back to our home. I asked Lisa where she lived, and if she wanted to go there. She said, yes, and gave me directions, "It's right there, and well, it's not much, but it's home." I would fully understand that statement in the years to come, but at the moment, I could not stand my so-called husband anymore, and I was in no hurry to get home.

Oh, boy, I was about to get some new education. Lisa lived with her boyfriend, a.k.a. pimp, who also sold drugs, and he became something of a teacher. No big surprise there, right!

After being introduced to Lisa's "Hookers' Book of Wisdom," I was shaking, and Lisa could tell she just scared the crap out of me. Casually, she said, "Do you need another hit?" "God, yes," I replied. After I stopped trembling, I thanked Lisa for the schooling and told her that I would talk with her again soon; maybe. I drove back home because Jared was waiting for me to take him to work.

In the end, this was how I had found my way into "that" world and the people out there who moved around in the shadows. Those predators waiting on the more fortunate people to come out and pick up their vice of the night. The drug dealers and hookers set on servicing your every wish... for a price. The streets I had traveled for Jared would end up being the same place I would continue to support my habit and stay high on my terms, or so I thought. That dark place of secrets and destruction for so many souls and a world filled with unending self-torture was right out in the open and beckoning me. Jared got his second DUI only a few weeks after clearing up the consequences of the first. The courts ordered him to stop drinking, driving, or using drugs for the next five years. The fun was over and he realized that if he was caught again he wouldn't drive for the rest of his life, so he complied with the sentence given him. Jared had been forced to stop while I continued to stay high. Being Jared would be drug tested weekly and wear an ankle monitor for the next five years, he would be the better choice for our kids' well-being and future than with my Ma, in West Texas. As I let go of any hope of ever having a real home and family with Jared; it was beyond impossible.

However, there was a dream I still held fast to, I remembered how I escaped from destruction in my past. In my lucid moments, I explored how I might possibly do it again. I remembered hearing once, "Where there was a will, there was also a way."

I didn't know if I could find that strength again, but it was something that was always in the far reaches of my mind.

Take a moment, and try to imagine the abuse I had endured for me to feel and believe that the only way I could have a better life, at this time and place, was to go live on the streets and get high? I accepted that I had failed myself and God so completely that the fight I once had was now gone. Maybe God wouldn't be able to save me, from myself and there wasn't any real guarantee that He was listening to me right now. Drugs were all that was important to me now, even worse than before, and 'more' was not enough. The potent drugs had distorted my mind. All of my achievements, career, family, home, business, and all the niceties of life the hard work and diligence to obtain it, however brief, passed through my mind, and I accepted they were probably gone forever. In a blink of an eye, this was the cost of staying drunk and high. It had so insidiously begun and had become all that was important to me, at any cost, right down to my self-respect and mortal life. The extremes I had let myself be drawn into plummeted me steadily, ever deeper into pathological despair from which so few ever avoid its fatal outcome. I was addicted mind, body, and every part of my being to drugs.

It was questionable whether my soul was a prisoner of these substances; only science and faith would have that answer. I was too depressed and mentally fragmented to know that answer for myself. I had been living in a deviated state for so long, so I could barely remember what my former, rational self, was about and how to live any kind of life where drugs were not an essential part of my day. Was I, in simplest terms, suffering the effects of self-directed brainwashing? Due to the severe and prolonged effects of the drugs I was consuming, was I permanently living in a delusional, hallucinatory state of consciousness from which there would be no return?

Another question, with a fuzzy image accompanying it, came and went more than once in recent months; would I live to explain to my kids what happened to me and to them? Most days, when the question crossed my mind, I was not really sure.

I remember I had been given opportunities for much-needed recovery during the last couple of years, but I had totally ignored them. Was it God I was ignoring or just well-intended people who encountered me but whom I also had no faith or belief in? At this point, the drug psychosis had derailed my perceptions and my rational mental functions that I was no longer sure I even needed any help. Perhaps I was such a mentally gifted person, even with horribly altered and diminished mental capacities, that I was able to avoid the declaration of complete, life-threatening, drug psychosis which allowed me to avoid forced incarceration in a rehabilitation facility, strapped to a bed, given anti-psychotic meds intravenously until I was less suicidal. Perhaps, if I had done so, I would not have gone to the streets and served all that jail time. These questions we will revisit a little later.

Yes, God did send help to me, but I was not acknowledging any of it, because I wasn't ready to try. I would later discover and understand, with professional guidance, that my unconscious, animal-survival instincts were making my decisions. Jared tried to get me help a few times, but he too was afraid someone would discover how bad things really were and how the kids were living under such conditions. So, he lied. Telling the truth could have changed the treatment plan and my fate could have been altered. My clever and extremely strong will, built from years of enduring the harsh forces in my earlier childhood, prevented anyone from penetrating my defenses and gaining my trust, that might have been there to aid and further my recovery.

Instead, I sat meekly and held fast to my inner world of defenses; I kept at bay the helping hands that wanted to reach me and pull me back. During one of my visits in the treatment ward of the hospital, I watched the others who were dressed in hospital garb like me. I viewed orderlies scurrying about desperately trying to keep everyone calm while others, not as fortunate as I, were sitting in wheelchairs lost in their own minds and barely able to walk anymore. I simply kept quiet hiding safely behind a wall in my own mind. After a few weeks in the hospital, the staff believed I was ready to go home; I was discharged and ready for more destruction. This routine would be repeated again a mere six months later for drug rehab with a similar outcome. It seemed to be a vicious cycle of me relapsing into a deep, dark depression, then treatment, and then readmitting me into my own home, or rather my prison.

A short time after my thirtieth birthday, I was admitted again for treatment and rehabilitation for chronic depression. No one was able to penetrate my defenses or know that getting high had become an organic mode of survival for me. None of the doctors available to treat me had the advanced knowledge required to understand and treat a condition most often seen and treated in soldiers who had adapted to long-term battle fatigue and the same illnesses in prisoners housed and hidden away in prisons across the United States. It was never revealed in public literature but available only to a small group of specialists and researchers in the medical community. None of them ever heard of Tiffany Rose Baker, unfortunately. Why had I not listened or took charge of my life? Why didn't I want to fight for my life anymore? These are the questions family after family cries out to their own loved ones who are lost in mental, behavioral, and drug/alcohol addictions or dysfunction. Loved ones who are awaiting treatment by a small group of about three dozen physicians among an estimated forty thousand patients needing treatment.

On a particular visit some years earlier to the psychiatrists', they revealed important facts about my mental acuity and the effects of consistent drug use by strong-willed people with unusual personality traits and learning styles. So too would a series of events that would closely follow. I was never fully aware of hidden characteristics that were both a blessing and a curse to me.

After the usual small talk about how I was adjusting to my new meds and if I was eating okay, the doctor got right to business. "You knew you were pregnant, but the drug use didn't stop?" the doctor asked me. "Yes, I knew. I wanted to stop. I tried. I tried really. Jared made me feel so bad and worthless. I was able to stop for a few days when I knew how far along in the pregnancy I was. Enthusiastic I was sure I could stay clean, but after a few days and then a few weeks, I just didn't feel like having sex anymore, and I didn't want to do some of the things he kept demanding I do with other women, and he made me feel horrible. I was just going to do a little more for a day or two, maybe just a little, and I would be able to get clean. However, he brought some other girl home one night when he was high and drunk, and I came home and found them in our bed. I wanted to kill myself; it felt so bad. I didn't want to lose my husband, and I didn't know what to do."

"So you knew you were pregnant, and your husband knew you were pregnant and he didn't support you being clean for the baby? Is that correct, is that what you are saying?" she asked quietly. "Yes," I responded. For a few moments, I realized how wrong my actions were. I was pregnant with an innocent child, and I was using drugs. A little, then a little more, and then it was every day again. Why? Why? Why didn't Jared see that it was wrong? I was carrying his child too. Why didn't he care? Why couldn't he see he had to help me? Couldn't he just stop for a while and be happy I was giving him a baby that he said he really wanted? Couldn't he just be my husband and not some other stranger's sexual playmate while we were having a baby?

We were supposed to be 'family'.

"Dr. Beth, I said just before I walked out of her office, I think I'm ready to try and maybe I can get Jared to help me this time. Maybe he can see our family is important and that I want to have sex only with him and not threesomes and other kinky stuff."

Two days later I was released from the hospital and went right back to my using. A few days later, with so little self-control over my life, I crashed the new car Jared had bought for me shortly after a trip to rehab the last time, in a head-on collision with another car. I had little Johnnie in the car with me while I had been out getting high. I was racing to pick up Crystal from preschool long after her dismissal time and I was high as a kite, it was pouring down rain, and the roads were slick. I never saw the other car before it was too late. I had told myself, "This was it; one last time." Nonetheless, awakening in the ER, I realized there never could be just "one last time" without a fatal ending more likely than not. This relapse almost cost my son's life, and now Jared was scared of the monster that had taken over my soul. Too little, too late, but Jared did finally get a conscience after his son was born and realized what he had done to me and how it added to my already shattered life.

I completed my second rehab inpatient program before I finally took to the streets. Everyone was praying that a quick, thirty-day stint in a drug program was going to fix everything, but could it fix that which had been broken inside me for a very long time now, was the question? The facility where I received my introduction to the 12-Step program of Alcoholics Anonymous and Narcotics Anonymous way of life which included learning to trust in a Higher Power; I was also told that if I just did not use then life would be all better. This was totally insufficient to treat my addiction, and honestly, it's inaccurate for the majority of addicts, just ask them.

I tried my best and put in the effort I thought was needed; I soon realized my recovery was going to require time and work. I sat for four weeks listening and watching but remained feeling isolated by all going on around me; the fear I lived with all my life was more obvious now than ever, and emerging was the realization that I was socially inept. Fear kept me from socializing with others; so I did my little assignments and tried to play some volleyball or cards during that bit of free time structured into the day's routine. But none of the factual data made any real impact on me or any of us honestly. So how can we bring in an element to recovery where those suffering can see, feel and touch, true inspiration about a new life and how to get there.

Why did I and others do this to ourselves? My answer to the question today has two parts. The first is simply because it's easier, and two, and perhaps more important for recovery is that true and lasting recovery must address underlying emotional issues or reasons that support a destructive addiction. Responsibility for our addiction and its effects more often than not will REQUIRE dealing with and eliminating unresolved conflicts or the rationalizing of our addiction to reach and maintain sobriety. It won't often be easy even with skilled professional help to get to the core issues that most often underlie a majority of our addictions. Addicts without this knowledge and at least partial solutions that identify the conflicts and empower control over the addiction of choice rarely reach true lasting sobriety from addiction. I can partially illuminate this dilemma from my experience and other addicts who contributed to my understanding of the problem and the medical professionals who have guided us at various times in recovery.

Being I didn't have to make any of those hard choices or change to measure up to what the rest of the world was doing. I avoided Responsibility, yeah, that's what it's called, and that's what I began to believe.

A medical mystery that remains to baffle the best medical minds that are trying to find treatments for people who suffer such as myself. I remember back in my teenage years when self-discipline and willpower for self-improvement were constant and consistent. Do you remember how I made hard choices and necessary, solitary, sacrifices to excel in sports, swimming, skating, auto mechanics, and my waitress work? That was really who I was and who I was proud of being. I almost lusted for personal achievement. Remember the journey through electronics school and the success on the factory floor in unknown territory? Alcohol and weed barely phased my capacity to achieve because I really wasn't consuming the excessive amounts I later realized were small.

The mystery that experts are still in search of is to identify an exact and precise biochemical or organic understanding of what happens in the brain and to the personalities of so many high-flying Wall Street folks and other high profile, high achieving, professionals who abuse drugs and alcohol. This list includes far too many outstanding athletes and doctors; people who suddenly, and without warning, permanently lose their natural achievement motivation that served them so well. For nearly everyone who did or does much cocaine, the answer is important for recovery. A real, usable answer, if it's discovered in time, can restore the potential for full recovery in so many thousands that struggle with regaining their will to recover and make themselves whole again. The medical journals and thousands of research papers still reveal a few useable clues to this elusive element of addiction recovery.

Because cocaine had stolen my most valuable gift, my power to believe in my own ability, and the will to overcome much of anything, I was not unlike a blind man or woman holding a book in front of their face, believing he can read the book, and cure his blindness. It's not an absurd statement, it's an abstract reality of a mental function that many say is what the soul provides a faithful believer, but that means believing in a soul even existing to empower self-control and resolve underlying conflicts that initiate or sustain addiction.

For me, my Higher Power did prove important to my recovery from addiction when I did chose to recover. Not recovering is also a choice, and I was still making that choice at my 12-Step introduction because it was the easiest, least painful way to avoid digging deep and opening Pandora's box of pain and self-doubt. I carried on with my drug use instead of seeing the answers right in front of me... because even before finding my way to Dixie Highway and hooking, I had all the tools I needed to recover and stop using. But, I was simply way too tired and too weakened by emotional fatigue and organic deficiencies, so I continued on with my own self-inflicted, self-medicating torture which just seemed, given my impaired condition, to be easier.

There were times when I returned home from rehab after being clean for a few weeks, and Jared would use that old famous line most of us think we can get away with, "Just this one last time, I know how to handle it now."

Telling myself that was the biggest joke we all tell ourselves
because it is the
– 'BIG TRAP!'

Jared would say, "Come on Tiffy, get high with me tonight. One night won't get you hooked again." So onto that Ferris Wheel, I would go once again, just weeks into another try at recovery. I had let Jared prey upon my weakness and guilt to deny me the freedom I actually wanted. Now, all that was left could only be an endless game of cat and mouse chasing after my drugs and elusive high.

6

IT AIN'T A VICTIMLESS CRIME

That FIRST night...
was a crash course in turning tricks, getting high, and all the violence it held.

Into Wonderland or was it *Horrors Ville*, I go.

It all just seemed to run together. Sex, drugs, and rock-n-roll weren't at all what they were cracked up to be. Because no matter what, well unless of course that you die from using, you will eventually have to stop. Even with all those worldly things and plenty of knowledge on how to stop, I was just too lost and never saw the need to change; I could have saved myself years of pain. I had all the tools to overcome my battle; I received them back there in one of those facilities, designed to help-me-help-myself. Unfortunately, my lack of desire and fear of leaving Jared to reclaim my freedom on my own, I was thrust into the jungle with the beast.

I remember when Lisa, the last sex toy Jared brought home before his second DUI, had laid it all out for me that morning when I took her home. She explained all about the dynamics and the hierarchy of street life, the different types of tricks she dealt with, and why she had a pimp instead of just being out there all alone.

Lisa's "Hookers' Book of Wisdom" goes something like this:

The Stroll was where we spent most of our time. We walk while the sun's heat radiates off the hot pavement beneath our feet, as we meander down Broadway hoping to catch another trick. The smell of the hot air hits us hard as we try to breathe in this humid mix of vapors burning our lungs and watch the cars driving by slowly, looking for that slight glance of interest. Yes, we are appalled that we are still out here trapped by years of the shame we feel, but we get that money and head straight for the dope boys to ease those horrible feelings from what we experience and endure.

Drug dealers stand huddled on their assigned corners up and down the street set back in just a bit from the main road. Posting up on 15th Street and E Ave all day long was Lisa's pimp, Peanut, a short guy not much bigger than her. Up close near the old run-down house that was long ago boarded up, the smell of urine was stifling and the overgrowth of the bushes against the ragged porch gave Peanut good cover. It offered a great view of the oncoming traffic up the street revealing a potential buyer driving up in their Benz or the cops rolling by just to make a showing in the area.

Just over a block away was the small bar that the dope boys hung out in when they needed to get out of the heat or the prying eyes of the cops; it was a place they met the upper-level guys to re-up their supply or plot a drive-by for the rival gang in the next city down the road. They also did their recruiting and training nearby or out front if need be, and we girls were not allowed anywhere near the place according to Lisa.

This is how it all works: the suppliers come from out in the sugar cane area of Okee where they cook up the drugs, and no one complains as the toxic fumes filter in the air. A small farming town with no work and major crime makes for the perfect cover of an illicit substance. Profit from sales was sent back to Okee where it was stuffed in hollowed-out oranges and grapefruit and sent out of state to be laundered and then back to the Kingpin. It was a military or business hierarchy with a General or CEO being in charge of the movement and timing of all distribution.

The dealers also had rank as the Lieutenant or Captain would be in charge of street distribution procedures; once the drugs were ready for delivery, they would either go out to Okee or meet up in a hotel in a neighboring city for the handoff. They also had to distribute the drugs and keep tabs on who was getting how much, exchange money from the last shipment, and bring the product to the street-level guys. These guys were the Sergeants and in charge of smaller amounts for street sales; they were also in charge of the girls who were going to spend hours with some trick, a.k.a. 'John', who had lots of time and money to spend. The Sergeants had to keep an eye on the corner boys to make sure they weren't using more than they were selling so they could make a profit of their own allowing them to feed their habit or their families. These guys were out there day and night; someone was always on duty unless, of course, they knew about a sting or the drugs were sold out, and they were waiting for a new supply to come in from out West.

I was shaking by this point, being introduced in the Hookers'

Book of Wisdom and she could tell that she just scared me and says casually, "Do you need another hit?"

"God Yes," I replied. Lisa continued explaining all this to me, as she said; "then there's the trick's like your husband Jared, sorry." I said, "Don't be sorry, I've been getting more accustomed to it for a long while now." Before asking her to tell me more.

There are three types of tricks and each one of them is dangerous in its own way. First, #1: is The Rich Guy – He doesn't want to be alone while he's getting high and just wants to have his limp dick sucked while he is smoking crack or meth, snorting a line, or shooting up. These are the easiest for us, work-wise, but they are so paranoid so you must always stay on guard. And, #2: The Family Guy or Single Guy – He is in a weak or bad relationship and needs to blow off steam with a quick blowjob or screw in his car. Maybe we do it in the parking lot, at the Save-a-Lot, the graveyard, or he pulls off the side of the road in some neighborhood late at night. Driving is always annoying because it takes them much longer to get off. And lastly, #3: The Freak – He is the guy who wants to save us and take us home to be his wife. There is also the guy who is just twisted, wanting to kill for the fun of it, enjoys violence, and is looking for it; the guy you know immediately after getting in the car with him that you need to get out in a hurry, even if it means opening the door while the car is moving and *JUMP!* Lisa warned me about staying away from the local boys with an ugly story of her own. "I was desperate one night. Things were slow on the Stroll, and I was hurting for a fix. I had done a couple of tricks early and was able to buy, but I got some really bad stuff, weak as hell, made me sick. I went back out to make a score a few blocks away from my place and was just really hobbling along when a local car I had seen before stops, and the nice-looking guy, well, really a boy, asked me if I needed a ride. I was, like major out of it, you know, but relieved because I figured he was a local and alright; so I climbed in the car. Girl, what he did to me, no john ever even asked me for, before or since. The cops found me early in the morning, lying naked on the bank of the canal over by the Knight's Inn. I woke up in the ER a couple of days later, and I was still in bad shape. Cut, bruised everywhere, and messed up pretty bad down below. I didn't remember some of what he did to me that night for a couple of weeks because the doctors said I had a concussion. I was, you know, sodomized pretty bad, and I didn't heal for almost a month because I had to have stitches, too. Don't ever get in a ride with any of the local guys because they think you ain't nothing but trash to throw out. You know what I mean. Wide-eyed I just shook my head yes with fearful understanding.

A few nights after receiving Lisa's street-life wisdom, I needed to get high and felt frightened and alone when the cravings to use could not be fought anymore. I left Jared sleeping with the children and went to the streets in search of some drugs. A nervous, thirty-year-old, computer tech mommy who loved to get high more than she loved herself or her family willingly stepped off a cliff, never thinking about what the consequences would be, and fell right down into an abyss. This was the fateful night that I decided to leave my family and run off into my own Never-Never Land. The following three days would be brutal; the thirty days after would bring me my first felony and a life-altering path, and it would be almost ten years before I would see the error of my ways.

I parked my car in the driveway of the local motel down on Dixie Highway where the working girls took tricks and the dope boys passed thru to distribute their product. The ever-present pimps were watching me while they were making sure everyone was being paid, and the muscle was there also to enforce it all ran smoothly. I only vaguely remembered Lisa's warning about the locals when I left the room I had just rented and walked a few blocks out onto the Stroll for my first attempt to get picked up by a guy who was looking for some action. I walked a half hour before a car I had seen parked at my motel stops along beside me, and a guy yells out the window, "I got the good stuff, baby, and I got the money, too, if you want to play a little while."

I hesitated for a moment, but knew I had to start somewhere

and stepped off the sidewalk and climb into the car. I didn't see the two guys in the back seat before it was too late, and instantly I had too many arms holding me to prevent me from an escape. I felt cold inside and went limp. Terror struck me deep when they rounded the corner a few blocks away and pulled into the driveway of a house deep in the hood. Hours of torture began and kept coming while I was gang-raped, at least twice, by each of the three of them. They slapped, punched, and brutalized me while they laughed and high-fived each other. I begged them, "Don't hit my face!" as I kept my arms up to block any fists that may come my way. If only they would give me some dope, I thought, I would be able to tolerate some of what they were dishing out. I plead, "I need a hit! Where's the drugs you said you had for me?" They laughed harder at me.

By the time the last boy was finished with me, my body ached, and I felt sure there was permanent damage somewhere in or on my beaten body. They drove back towards the place they had grabbed me and stopped the car long enough to shove me onto the pavement just short of the sidewalk… the gutter. After a few minutes, I forced myself to stand, but could barely walk without feeling extreme pain. No drugs, no money. My introduction to the life of a prostitute had already left me literally in the gutter, and I hadn't even done my first trick yet, but I had been raped… again.

I had to get high, and now my body needed it to combat the pain just inflicted on me. I needed some money badly, to buy the drugs and pay the motel charges. Finding the strength to work my way back the few blocks to my room, I carefully sneak in to see how bad I looked then clean myself up; I numbly forced myself back to the Stroll in less than an hour. Ten, fifteen, twenty minutes go by, and as many cars before I say, "Thank God," when an old man pulled up and signaled me over. I got in the car not knowing or caring if he might just blow my brains out; I needed money, right now, to get high at any cost. The gray-haired, well-dressed gentleman, driving a nice Caddy made me feel a little safer, and I forced the best smile I was capable of at the moment.

He asked if I was okay seeing that I was shaking a bit. "Yes, I'm fine. Just a little excited," I lied boldly with another smile. He smiled back, and said, "Well, I guess I am too, then. I have a little, quiet place we can go park if fifty dollars will do for it."

"Will you bring me back here," I ask quickly. "Sure." He responds. "Yes, okay," I said, being in no mood to quibble about his low, fifty-dollar offer for the BJ because I needed anything right at the moment.

Thirty minutes later, I got out of the Caddy right where I had gotten in, feeling something new. An ugly and disgusting feeling that would not go away anytime soon, and not like those feelings of self-hate I had while watching Jared with his other girls. This was my first real exchange of sex for money, and just for a second, I almost felt bad enough to never do it again, but at that moment, the cravings overcame the morals, and I had the money to get high. I went straight to the nearest street dealer I could spot. As the pain eased and the high grew, I was feeling better about where I was and hit the stroll for another date. I had been on these same streets plenty over the last year bringing girls home after Jared used them. I had gone out and bought drugs on these dark streets alone late at night because Jared really was a jerk and had sent me out to risk my life to get them. Now, I would have to learn how to shut off those feelings every time I serviced some john.

I went back to the motel room and grabbed my few belongings, I decided to work from my car for a few days, so I could use the room money to buy drugs instead. I parked my car a couple of blocks off the Stroll and set off to begin another round of my new job. Within a few minutes, I caught the look I was waiting for from a middle-aged guy in a Lincoln; it was a virtual repeat of the trip in the Caddy. We had driven a little farther and took a few minutes more getting back, but I had upped the price to seventy-five dollars when he asked thinking he couldn't say 'no' very easily while driving a nice Lincoln and looked the part.

Getting back to where my car was parked, I rested a few minutes then got out. Looking to buy some dope, I walked up to a guy leaning against the wall of the motel I had recently vacated. I scored the dope and eased the pain I had been looking to fix hours ago; it was the best high I could remember in a long time. A half-hour later, I was back out on the Stroll looking to catch another trick, get a handful of money, go buy more drugs and get high to escape the new pain added from this life I had begun to lead.

The vicious cycle continued as I, more nervous than before, asked a different dope boy if he could get me a couple dimes. Little John replied, "Yeah sure, No problem. Just follow me down the street to my car." We had been walking half a block when he turned and said in a reassuring voice, "We are almost there baby and it's good stuff. You'll see. Just follow me." We walked another block, and I began thinking about turning around and walking back the way I came to find another dealer when he said, "Right in here," as he turned into a dirty alley between two buildings.

Before I could ask where was the car that I was expecting, he spun around and grabbed the back of my head with one hand, and with the other, put a long sharp blade up tightly to my throat. I froze and felt my whole body begin to tremble and squeezed myself inside to stop from peeing my pants.

"Scream, bitch, and you die! Give me ALL the money, and I won't cut you too deep," he said with a low growl as he pulled my face close to his and looked into my wide eyes; I could smell the stench of his breath. I was stunned and surprised by the suddenness of his movements as he backed me into the wall and pushed the knife harder into my throat, and I felt the warmth of my urine flowing down my legs. There are no words to describe that helpless feeling when you know death was surely coming. "Okay," I whispered, "I will, I will!"

Little John snapped, "Give me what you got stashed, too. I know you got more! Come on, quick, give it up or I'll cut you open." I reached into the pocket of the hip hugger shorts, pulled the folded bills out, and held them up where he could see them. He snatched the money away, and put his face an inch from mine, and glared into my eyes. "All of it, bitch, I told you. I know you got more money. Give it up," he snarled. "Okay, I will," I pleaded, "It's in my shoe. There's another hundred in my shoe; it's all I have! I swear, I swear!"

"Alright then, you gonna bend down slowly and take them shoes off, and there better be a hundred dollars in there, and you better not try to run or your gonna die." He took a step back, and I slowly bent down, pulled off my right shoe, and extracted the folded hundred dollar bill it contained, and without raising up, handed it up to him. He snatched it from my hand, and said, "Take off the other one, bitch, I ain't kidding you, bitch. You better give me all the money." I took off the other shoe, and I could see it was wet from where my urine had run down my leg and held it up for him to take from my trembling hand.

I watched as he looked into it and shook it to see if any more money would fall out while his eyes darted from mine to the shoe. "Alright now," he said with a weak smile forming on his face. "Get up slow and easy. We gonna find out if you holding out on Little John." I shakily raised myself off the ground and leaned back against the wall, knowing there was no way I could get away from him fast enough to avoid his knife and knew screaming wouldn't bring anyone quick enough to stop him from killing me with it.

With one hand, he reached in and pulled my two-button blouse open, exposing my bra-less breasts, while waving the knife back and forth with the other. "Okay, then. Do you got some more money in there in your p..sy? Tell me now, and save your life cause if you do, I gonna cut that pretty face for lyin' to me. Pull them pants down, and show me the money-maker right now," he said. "I don't have anymore. Please, I am telling the truth. I gave you all the money I have, I swear. You have all my money just let me go, and I won't ever say anything, I swear," I pleaded. "Baby, I told you. Pull down them pants, and show me the stash you got in there right now."

"Okay, okay. I will," I said. With badly shaking hands, I undid the snap and the zipper of the hip huggers and slid them down my hips low enough for him to see there was no more money in my pants. For what seemed hours, he stood there with the knife waving back and forth and an unnerving smile staring at my exposed breasts and vagina. I was more scared than I had ever been in my life, and the tears of fear, shame, and the thought of dying in a dirty ally while trying to score drugs began to flow uncontrollably. I started sobbing, and my hands went to my face as I slid unsteadily down the wall, falling hard on my buttocks with my pants still down almost to my knees.

Was this my life story?

I cried and sobbed with hands covering my eyes for I don't know how long. Maybe it was just minutes or maybe it was hours. The weather was gloomy, and darkness was fast approaching. I finally lifted my head to see if he was still standing there flashing a knife around and wanting to end my life. When I was certain he wasn't just around the corner counting the money and waiting for me to move, I got up cautiously, pulled up my pants, and closed my blouse. I was still alive and didn't see any blood, so I assumed the nightmare was over. I wanted to run, and run quickly, but I was uncertain what might await me outside the ally. Was he, or even someone else, waiting to kill me? Was it safe to go back the way I came, or should I find another, hopefully, safer, passage back to my car? I had no money and no coke, and I was totally alone; I knew I had been stupid to fall for such a play. But. I was alive, and I knew if I didn't get the hell out of there while it was still light something worse might happen. I took a few cautious steps out of the ally, found the sidewalk, and looked around to see if he might be waiting to silence me so he won't get caught. In my haste, I had forgotten my shoes, but I wasn't looking back or going back. I began to run.

No, I wasn't thinking about getting home as fast as I could, I was thinking about how to get high. Still, after all that... getting high was the only priority.

Yes, a normal person would have run for safety immediately to stop the madness.

> Not Me. — An addict will go to *any extreme to get high*, and yes. I was very much a desperate addict by now.

It was time for some protection to help make sure nothing like this happened again. My new friend, Teresa, and I were hanging out and talking in the park by the marina in Seaside the next day. I told her that Jared had finally found my car and had it towed, so now I was really trapped. I had found this world appealing – the drugs and the easy money – because there were plenty of perverts, like Jared, to go around.

They were here, and they came out in the middle of the night when no one else could see. The judges, lawyers, doctors, writers, and professionals of all sorts, plus there were your average every day, Joe or Jane. The new life I had embarked upon, I quickly realized, was a cold existence. Not even the thoughts of my kids could keep me from the desire to stay high. My moral compass was lost, and my neurosis and the compulsion for easing the pain with the drugs was gripping the very core of who I was now. I would recount my recent experiences to Lisa one night soon and confess to her my misconceptions of what the street life would be about and what I had learned so far.

"I had blindly and smugly believed in my own ability to perceive any danger or threat I was going to encounter; it was going to be easy, or so I thought. I could offer up whatever they wanted, put a price on it, take their money, do what I had to do, and be on my way. Five minutes, ten minutes, maybe twenty, and I had enough cash to get high again and be in my comfort zone for however long the trick's money could buy me. Get in, ride a few blocks to a lightly traveled side street, tell the guy to pull over, get it done quickly, get out with my money in hand, and buy a small bag from a street dealer as I walked back to the stroll. Or maybe direct the guy over to the marina on a weekday when there were plenty of empty spaces, or if the guy was worried about being stung by the cops in a neighborhood known to be frequented by hookers plying their trade, the edge of the big mall parking lot a few miles away. If it could be done in a car, then that was the routine and the usual way of doing business with the "nooners." What they wanted, was a quickie or oral sex on their lunch break or while they were on their sojourns between the office and home, or between their office and the courthouse, or seeing one customer and another if they were salesmen, et cetera. These guys were the successful, middle-aged, married professionals with spare time in their busy schedules, and money in their pockets to do as they pleased when the opportunity presented itself."

My girl, Teresa, had her own humorous, although serious revelations about the "nooners." She was blunter with her explanation, but she spoke the truth, "All you got to do, girl, to get it done is be in the right spot at the right time. Be ready to take a quick ride around the block with the "nooner" so you get that regular money your main man is gonna want from your ass every day. It's that easy, and you can do it cause there is more of them than there is of you or us.

It also means you got some regular business right from the get-go, too, if you want it." Teresa assured me for future reference, that hardly ever on a Monday, but Tuesday thru Friday the "nooners" could be counted on to be horny and search for it at least a couple times a week, and they could also be counted on as regulars. She was all business about the business of hustling and wanted me to know how to do it better than what I had been doing. The other more serious sexual stuff she would explain in sordid detail a little later she said. So, she hooked me up with a pimp for my own good.

Teresa says, "Tiffy did you hear me? I said, it's time to go; we gotta meet Kevin and give him his money." My new pimp, Kevin, loved all the money I was making, and he had a serious thing for me. He was all about the money and protecting it at all costs. Besides racking up and stashing some of the money, I took good care of myself even though I stayed as high as I possibly could to drown out the noise of my own sadness. Kevin would line up his girls for a beat-down regularly just so no one forgot that he was in charge out here, and we all answered to him. Kevin was a very mean bastard, but he had quickly fallen for innocent, emotionally immature me and had his soldiers always following close by to keep watch.

One day, Teresa and I went to the Fish House, an old fishing warehouse in the marina, where a lot of the crowd hung out to get high and bought drugs out of sight from the cops, I made some woeful new discoveries. Meth for the tweakers, crack for the crackheads, and heroin for the needle lovers who liked to nod. As we walked in we noticed that Kevin was pacing back and forth, and without warning, grabbed Teresa and slammed her into the wall, leaving an imprint of her body in the old drywall.

He screamed, "Bitch, why am I standing here waiting on you? I told you to be here ten minutes ago!" Still stunned from the impact of hitting the wall, all she could do was look up at him as she tried to catch her breath. He turned to me, and bellowed, "You! Do you finally have my money? This ain't no charity show up in here."

I dug the six, twenty dollar bills out of my pocket and hand them to Kevin. I watched as Teresa tried to stand up and ready herself for another assault from him. Teresa was digging into her own pocket for the money she owed Kevin as he turned to her in a rage. Barely looking him in the eye, Tee handed him three-hundred dollars, and begged, "Please, Big Papa, don't hit me again." She paused only a heartbeat before asking him if she could get a 20 bag of rock. "Big Papa" was what everyone out on the streets called Kevin; he didn't let just anyone call him by his real name.

Calmer now that he had his money, Kevin said, "OK girls, here's your candy. Go take a little break, and I'll see you later. "Tee," he called Teresa, I want five- hundred by morning. It's Friday night, and it shouldn't be anything for you. And you newbie, I think I'll call you, Shorty Phat. I want two-hundred or else." We both just nodded yes, took our candy, and went to get high.

For now, Never-Never Land was going to be my new palace, and all this just to, just stay high... sad, right! Tell me, please, why would I do this to myself? The answer though was right there in that crack pipe, or at least, I thought it was the answer.

Nothing drove me harder than the relentless need to keep the pipe brimming and oblivion filling my mind. I had an insatiable need to take hit after hit, and never letting that high fall off for more than a few minutes. The amount I was consuming daily was already at a dangerous level, and this was just the beginning of my ten-year journey out here in Neverland.

It was about a week later that I found myself running into the next town to get away from Kevin and all his "protection." Who was he to tell me to stay close, and do what he said because it was for my own good? Did he know about something that I would soon learn?

I was apprehended during a drug sting for the low-level drug dealer I was hanging out with that night. Was it just the wrong place or the wrong time? Within one month on the streets, I had come full circle... from rape victim to a felon. The charge was drug trafficking with intent to sell. Lucky for me, if you could call it that, I had been there to buy, and it was a first offense. I was released on community control and went right back to the street. This fortuitous break should have been the wake-up call I needed, and I should have gone back home to my family and quit using drugs, but that was not the case.

A couple of weeks after being released, I caught a gun charge and knew what I would face going back to Kevin, and this is what happened. My plan was to find my way in with the main gang in the area of wpb. One night just as the sun was coming up, after that drug charge, I was in the hotel room with the local dope boy, Slime, when he stepped out of the room for a minute. Newly released from jail and high as hell, I got scared. There was a gun sitting on the dresser, and I had a bad feeling.

Slime said he would be right back as he stepped out of the room, and when an hour had gone by I knew it was time to go. Instead of just leaving the gun there, I picked it up and put it in my bag. Completely dumb, right? I figured if someone could identify me as leaving a gun in a motel room, I was screwed. Funny, because it probably was a setup anyway. As I was walking down the street with the gun in my bag, it never occurred to me that my rap sheet could get any worse than the pending felony charge and community control I had already been blessed with. No, I was still only thinking about more dope.

Four cop cars rushed in on all sides and surround me, God's blessing for me was the gun was unloaded, but surely not clean, and within six weeks of first stepping out onto the streets, yes, forty-two days, I became a felon for the second time and went to jail for a while. That gun must have been tied to some really bad action too because the Fed's came to talk to me about where it came from and wanted to make a deal with me for information. Luckily for me, all I could tell them was the truth which was; that I don't know whose gun it was, and I didn't want to leave it in an empty room for some kid to find.

I told them that it wasn't my room, and I didn't know anything about the guy. "So, do what you've got to do," was my last remark to them.

I was given six months in jail, and they took all the money I had on me at the time, about six hundred dollars, saying it was for court costs, et cetera. They ran the first felony probation in with the gun charge:

1st – Drug Trafficking w/ intent to sell   &   2nd – Possession of a Firearm

I had quite the resume' now, and all that within my first few weeks on the streets. This is when I was first introduced to Sister Ann's "Christian Life Skills" Drug Program as a patient/inmate. It would not be the last time that I would sit in a classroom trying to figure what went wrong. Something in my brain should have gone off, and screamed, "STOP!"

Unfortunately, I had to walk many more roads first, and they weren't going to be smooth. There wasn't anyone I trusted to help me get off this ride. Six months later, I was back on the street getting high; what else was I supposed to do? The only thing in my life that I knew for sure was that I was now a Felon and a drug addict who was just released from jail. All I wanted was to get high. All I kept thinking about while waiting to be released that morning was that I had walked away from Kevin, so I could not go back there.

When I stepped out of the jailhouse, onto that driveway, I saw it wasn't going to matter. Kevin was waiting for me, this time in his gold-colored Jaguar. I now was fully engulfed in this world of drugs and crime, so vile and treacherous a life that usually had only two preventable endings – prison or death. How did a successful computer tech, mommy by day, a drug addict by night end up here?

I was caught in a net of my own making.

As I walked up to Kevin's jag, the knot in my belly tightened; I leaned in through the window and give him a kiss on the cheek. I hoped he wouldn't drag my ass thru the window and beat the shit out of me right there in the parking lot of the jailhouse. Kevin said in his sweet voice, you know, that one that makes your skin crawl, "Tiff, get your ass in this car now; we got paper to go make."

After I hurried around the car and got in, Kevin handed me two big pill bottles full of crack, and said, "Stick them in your waist in case we get stopped," so I tucked them against my belly and prayed we got back across town quickly, so I could do a hit; I really missed that feeling of being high. I was also wondering as we drove back across town if it was my turn to get DEAD!

When he wasn't pimping girls or dealing drugs, Kevin a.k.a. Big Papa, a.k.a. Black Cat was a hired assassin.

The feds had just come to me about that gun, and I couldn't

help but be nervous about what might be coming next. I knew Kevin was pissed off, but he liked me for some reason, and I was his possession now. He often told me no one else was gonna have me but him or the graveyard. I truly knew that he meant it, too! I tried to relax as I kept an eye out for the cops.

Kevin took a left turn up Fifteenth Street to make a drop at the bar, so the boys could divide the product for the street distribution. Blue lights started flashing behind us out of nowhere, Kevin said, "Throw the bottles out the window," but I was too paranoid at this point knowing my prints were already on the bottles. So, I left them where they were and got out of the jag like the cops said to do when they came up to the window of the car.

I was scared but knew I couldn't show it. While standing there in a sports bra and skintight, size-six hip-hugger booty shorts, with my hands laying across my waist covering the pill bottles, I prayed. "God, I don't want to go back to jail today with two felonies already in a few short weeks' time. I'll be going away for many years, please Lord, don't let these cops touch me."

The cops frantically searched the jag, but I already knew there was nothing for them to find in the car. I also knew that they had no probable cause to search me. As the cop in front of me stepped back from the car and looked at me one last time, I could tell he was trying to decide if he was going to violate my rights or not, so I give him a big, flashing smile. Those few seconds seemed like hours as the cop stared at me, and I saw the other cop and Kevin staring at each other. I knew my fate lay in their hands; finally, the lead cop nods at Kevin and says they were sorry for stopping us, and we were free to go. The cop dropped his gaze from mine, turned, and walked back toward his cruiser. My gutsy, brave act of measured defiance and protection for one of the bosses down here in the game gave me the street cred that would keep me safe for the years ahead.

That next morning, I saw Teresa coming up the Stroll and could tell she was hurt. Helping Tee off the sidewalk into the shade alongside the thrift store, I hand her a bottle of water and said, "Tee what happened? You're pale as a ghost." Teresa began recounting her event as a warning about being cautious and careful when getting in a car with a customer. "The guy was agitated and nervous," she said, "More so than the average guy trolling the streets for a 'play,' but he was well-dressed and clean-shaven. The car and his face were unfamiliar. It was obvious when I leaned in through the window and he started talking that he seemed coked up and a little strung out. When I asked him what he wanted, he told me 'whatever five-hundred would buy'... I told him to 'show me the money.' He did so I got in; the money, I found out too late was fake bills. He stalled me while holding the money until we get to the marina. When we finished screwing and doing some of the coke I had, he said, 'Here take your money, bitch, and get out.' It wasn't until I had it in my hands and looked at it closely I realized the bills were fake."

"Tiff, Kevin is gonna kill me. I don't have his money or the drugs, I was holding for McCoy." Surprised, I asked, "You were you holding for McCoy?" Tee nervously explained what she had done. "I was on my way to drop it off because Kevin was in a hurry to get somewhere, and McCoy was running late. I thought I could make a few bucks and sit back to chill in McCoy's little shack for a bit. I violated the first rule, always get the money first."

I felt her pain and assured her that it would all work out. She should calm down and get out there to get that money quick before Kevin came looking for her. I was only too aware of the consequences when money wasn't earned or was lost. The number of lies, deception, treachery, and theft of money and drugs were a very large possibility just as were the consequences. When discovered, one could have terrible, and often fatal, consequences. I went on my way to make some paper, too, knowing I could have my own troubles if I didn't get mine. With a little bounce in my step, I began another stroll down Broadway. I was fresh meat for all the johns wanting to trick and escape their own worlds they too were running from. I pondered, as I stepped my strut, about the facets of my street life. The money flowed in bigger and better as I learned smarter strategies to conduct my business; I felt a special kind of cool about my new role. Not that it was anything to be proud of, but it was now my life, and I was going to be the best as possible at it. It was like waitressing, but with a different menu, at least that's what I believed in my disillusioned state of mind. With the ever-increasing amount of money I was earning doing tricks and moving the drugs along, the other girls started resenting me. There was also a little outright hatred from repeat male customers because I could take their money, with their consent, so easily and so often. Some customers outright resented me after I did their bidding, blaming me, and would try to give me in some holier than thou guilt trip to make themselves feel better.

I would look at all the beautiful cars slowly rolling down the street, with people in them that had thoughts more perverted than you could probably imagine. I would make eye contact with those that I could sense their purpose and give a little smile to intrigue them. Bingo, around the block they would come even faster than the last time they'd picked me up. My hazy arrogance about it all sometimes left me ignorant of the real danger I was putting myself in. All that mattered was stacking money and getting high with no one to answer to for my actions.

On a slow afternoon, I met up with Teresa and shared a recent event that highlighted the danger of my growing indifference to how fast things can go wrong with a john. As I was drinking a bottle of water leaning against a wall out of the grinding heat, I explained one of my more recent experiences.

"It was clear there was no way to talk my way out of what was coming. With little forethought about what might be in the mind of the middle-aged, coat and tie professional, I had climbed in the car figuring he wanted sex. The guy was angry and felt cheated. The difference between what he had expected for his money and what he said he wanted and paid me for was very different. He had gotten his usual "afternooner" after a five-minute ride to the outer fringe of the mall parking lot. Therefore, I was completely unprepared and very surprised when he put the gun into view and glared at me with a cold, beady-eyed look that told me he would love to hurt me just for the fun of it.

Then he grabbed me and pushed the gun to my head, and this whack job says, 'Give me another BJ.' We drove out of the lot, and all the time we were riding I kept thinking, 'He's going to go through with killing me.' I begged him not to hit me in the face, and he didn't, but he pulled over and stopped the car. He then grabbed my head and shoved my face in his crouch, and I felt the gun barrel on the back of my head. He starts repeating, 'Shut up and suck it.' My only thought was of getting back across town the minute this guy let me out of the car. So, I did him again, and then I started talking to him and telling him to just let me go, and I wouldn't tell anyone what happened. Was I ever freaking, but girl, I was also cold as ice calm. Finally, he drove me back closer to town, slammed on the brakes, and frigid as hell told me, 'Get the hell out of my car.' I got out and practically ran all the way back to my room, Tee."

Teresa shakes her head and gives me a pained look and then a smile. "Damn that's bad! Well gal look at the bright side of it, you are still alive to tell me the story ain't you? Don't get any better than that in my book except you didn't charge him enough for his funny little game! I have to get back to work. Now go on with it down the road, and get off my route." Teresa let out a hearty laugh, and I walked away. Both of us knew the laughter was a weak cover for the fear we both carried in our hearts when we walked the Stroll.

I began my own stroll a few minutes later while thinking about the limits of Kevin's protection in light of today's event. A few hours after getting out of jail last time, Kevin had given me his speech about listening to him, the boundary lines of his protection, and how much he cared about me immediately after he knocked my ass to the floor. I was so high and paranoid because it was that first high after being clean from my stay in jail. He was sincere, but he needed to make his point with brutal violence sometimes to make sure you were listening and paying attention. I got his message but knew now how easily I could become dead. A few days later, I would also understand he was almost powerless to protect me from my own self.

Strolling early one morning, I had gone into a narrow space between two buildings a little off Broadway to take a little hit from my crack pipe. Heart pounding and head spinning, I come out from the little hideaway feeling dizzy and begin to stumble. I knew what was coming, and I needed to be where someone could find me. Stepping down the sidewalk a few dozen steps, I was hoping the spinning would stop, but then the seizure hits me. I fell face-first into the road while seizing. I blacked out and crushed my right cheekbone, never feeling a thing. Luckily, God had been close by, and so was one of Kevin's soldiers. As he pulled me out of the roadway and up onto the sidewalk, all he could do was watch in horror and wait until it passed. It was 2 a.m., and there was not enough traffic for anyone to risk stopping in this neighborhood. Ty stayed with me until the seizure passed, and I woke up.

I saw a look of sheer terror in his eyes and bewilderment on his face about what had happened.

"What happened?

Where am I?" I asked in a slow slur.

"You had a seizure; I thought you were going to die," Tyrone says.

My rapidly swelling face was causing harsh pain, and through my bleeding lips I mumble to Ty," I need to get high to stop the ringing in my ears." Ty tells me, "Hell no, you can't do no such thing. Do you know what I just watched!" I did, but it mattered little. I was going to get high and no seizure was going to stop me.

I managed, with just a few words, to get Ty on his way, so I could do my thing, "Go get Kevin." I still had my stash in that favorite hiding spot on my body, so I picked myself up, went out of sight to hit on my pipe, and sat down on the sidewalk.

Ty met Teresa on his way to find Kevin and sent her to check on me. She arrived and grimaced when she saw my swollen face. "What the hell really happened to you? Did somebody do this to you, Tiff," she yelled. "No. I had a seizure and fell. Really."

"Ty said that, too, but I wasn't sure he was telling the whole truth," she told me help was on the way, and to just sit still until somebody got there. In a few minutes, one of Kevin's soldiers pulled up in a car with TY. They got me into the car, drove me back to my room, and got my face wrapped in a pillowcase filled with ice they had scooped from the machine in the lobby. After being satisfied that I would be okay, Kevin's soldiers depart leaving Teresa to observe me for a time. She was making small talk to keep me awake because she knew from experience what seizures were all about, so I had to stay awake for a while.

"I got a little teaching for you," Tee said. She begins to tell me about the "Dumb Tourist Type" john that almost got her killed. She explained that some DTT's are easy marks, but others are truly dangerous and smart. There was a way you could tell when you talk about what they want. So, recounting in great detail, her 'trick' identification skills, she actually made me manage a little laugh with my swollen face. I tell Teresa, "Well, with this mug today, I don't think even the quick, easy ones are going to be any fun to do. But, with enough candy, I guess I can go strolling in a little while. I don't need any like that gunslinger jerk I had the other day." Teresa asks me again if I was okay. I just looked at her, and said, "I'm okay, just need to get some more ice for my face and a little more candy, then I'll be fine."

What a sickening life I had grown comfortable living in.

Tee closed the door behind her leaving me lying on the bed with the ice bag covering my face. Within a few minutes, I sat up on the bed, and with the last bits from my stash, I started curling smoke in my pipe and decided it was past time to hit the Stroll.

7

THANK GOD FOR THE EMT'S

It was just a few days later a pair of EMTs, Charles, and Rick would find me in a crappy, pay-by-the-hour motel. They entered the room not knowing anything about who I was or what I had done. It was another distress call to a motel they knew were often frequented by partiers doing drugs and all the things that could go with them. I was face up, sprawled across the bed in bra and panties, and it was obvious I was in physical distress. I showed all the signs of another hard seizure. I was already slowly coming out of it by the time they arrived at my room. I could hear voices or sounds and sensed whatever was going on, was about me.

"Rick look. I think this crazy bitch is coming out of it.
Let's just watch her for a minute. Don't call it in yet."
"Okay, look, she's trying to sit up," said Rick.
I pushed myself to a sitting position, looking around the room and at myself before saying, "Hey guys, what's up? I mean listen,

seriously, I'm okay now. Thanks for coming so quickly, but I will be alright. You can go now. I don't want to go to any hospital."

Charles checked my pulse and eyes one last time to be sure they wouldn't be back in an hour calling for a coroner. He stared hard at me for a long minute, looked at Rick, and said, "That's it we're outta here." They had done all that was medically care required, and the legalities prevented them from violating any patients' rights. Having seen so many similar events, there was nothing else that needed to be done for this patient. I was more and more a walking zombie because I was staying high all the time to avoid any pain or turmoil going on emotionally. In reality, I was steadily going from really bad to much worse. Not to mention, were the below minimum thresholds of sleep I was surviving on. I didn't perceive the fatal danger that was immediately ahead on the path I was stubbornly following.

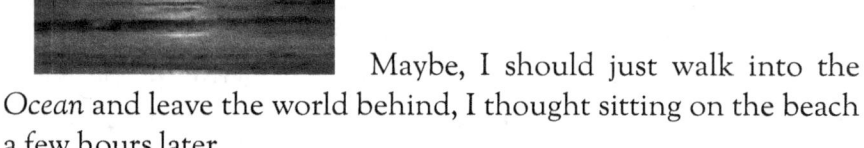 Maybe, I should just walk into the *Ocean* and leave the world behind, I thought sitting on the beach a few hours later.

I got my share of abuse from Kevin, but by his hand only. No one out there would think of touching me because they understood the pecking order of the streets and their rank in the army they belonged. Living with this small, but important, amount of respect from others allowed me to lessen the amount of work I did due to my steadily declining desire to engage in it, as the brutality was starting to wear on me.

The most troubling of several events close together was when Kevin sent me to a guy that wanted some backdoor action. After that brutal gang rape, it was the one thing I wouldn't do again, and I told the guy 'no'. Regrettably, I would soon find out that I really didn't have a say in what I was selling.

In a fury, Kevin burst through the door of my motel room and grabbed me while the look of rage on his face was unlike anything I had ever witnessed in my life. He picked me up like I was a toy doll and hurled my 130-pound frame across the small, dingy room. Having been up for the last week, I was easily dazed as I felt the weight of my body's impact with the floor snap my collarbone. Lying still and knowing better than to scream for help, I felt my limp body being lifted off the ground. Before I could blink, I was thrown onto the bed and staring at the ceiling. As I looked up at 300 pounds of brute evil, I pray to myself, "Lord help me."

I knew God heard my prayer for help because the next thing Kevin said was; "Take your ass to sleep. It's been a week, and you need to eat something, too." Grateful, I passed out the second he left, but within a few minutes, the pipe demon and the pain in my shoulder woke me. My addiction would again override my common sense and willpower to take care of myself; I gingerly eased myself off the bed and out the door.

When I reached the Stroll, my goal was to grab some quick action so I could buy the drugs I needed to take care of the pain I was feeling. I was so out of it that I barely heard this guy yell, "Hey!" through the car's passenger side window. He pulled up to the curb and asked if I was okay. In a daze, I stepped up to the car window and said, "Yeah I'm okay. I just fell earlier and my shoulder hurts." The dude told me to come get in the car, and he would take me to the hospital. I climbed in, and I sat there for a minute then told him to let me out at the next corner because I didn't want to go to the ER. He pulled over, and I saw the pain in this old guy's face as he watched me try to move my arm. I was opening the door to get out when I felt him grab my other arm lightly; when I turned to look at him, he handed me a hundred-dollar bill. I thanked him, like, ten times before I removed myself from his car completely; I was relieved I could go relax for a bit longer.

As I walked back to the room I called 'home,' I thought to myself that you just never know when God will send an Angel your way.

Over the next few years, the excessive pull of the drugs became horrifying and brutal, and the unpredictable seizures became much worse. In addition, to the unquenchable desire to use, the busted shoulder and torn ACL in my knee each added layers of pain and suffering because they affected me day and night. Standing, sitting, lying down, and all the other positions my work demanded were always painful, as the cold or rainy weather also contributed. It was unbearable, and all I could do to ease the pain was keep the pipe full almost constantly.

Tell me please, why would I do this to myself? The insatiable need to take another hit, never letting that high fall off for more than a few minutes, the amounts daily already near-fatal on the ten-year-long journey in Neverland. Pure unrestrained animal fear of the pain I couldn't control with a dysfunctional mind.

I am uncertain how or why I was able to function at all but regardless, I ate every day and drank plenty of water, I took care of my little room, I bathed almost excessively, and except for the obsessive amounts of drugs I used daily and sleep deprivation, I was just a regular person.

'Regular Person,' that was my horrible, completely – **psycho-pathological delusion** – that kept me on the tracks straight to Hell.

What made it all so easy and kept me on that track? The world is not at a loss for sad, lonely people aching to escape their own troubled lives. These people who will spend hundreds and thousands of dollars in one day to satisfy their own addictions. Rich guys that had the dope boy on speed dial and who would return weekly for their supply. These same guys would also spend big money on girls so they weren't alone as they got high.

Teresa said she really didn't have to perform much with these guys, as they really couldn't get it up for more than a minute or two after the first few hits, tokes, snorts, drinks, etc. The girls were there mostly to light the lighter, fetch a drink, or be able to call for more drugs when the supply ran out since the tricks were too high to drive anywhere. We were the delivery service. These '*whales*,' as Kevin and his pals liked to call them, were their prime and pampered customers that they were all about servicing. The pimps made available specific rooms for the girls to use so videos could be recorded. Kevin wanted to protect us, watch us, and extort money from these very rich guys. Whether it was fancy hotels or huge mansions on the ocean, I felt somewhat cool at first. What seemed glamorous in the beginning, soon became a sad, terrifying nightmare with no escape in sight.

Teresa told me about the nights she had spent with judges, lawyers, doctors, and rich guys from all walks of life, along with the whales that Kevin and his gang would set up to be serviced by Tee or any of his other girls in the stable. Yes, there were days that my habit kept me from functioning for more than a few moments before returning to the safety of my room to sit and watch television, smoke dope, and chill. However, on those other days, I entertained all of them and whatever their nasty vice was so they could pay for my $1000 a day crack habit. Clean coke, which preceded a crack addiction, was very expensive. These johns/tricks were all too happy to pay to keep us naked as we lit the lighter for them. The whole thing repulsed me, but the coke blinded me enough to keep me going back and degrade myself for it.

Early one morning, I was sitting in my room watching a little TV and smoking the rest of the drugs I had when there was a knock on my door. Teresa was standing there looking at me kinda strange so I let her in; she was mumbling something incoherent about a guy that wasn't worth the time or effort for the money he probably didn't have anyway.

She said, "What was even more likely was he hoping to steal

whatever I might have on me to put up his nose after pulling a knife or a gun and dumping me out of the car. That kind of thing happened to me more than once, and I didn't want to take the chance tonight." Then, Tee said, "I did take the chance and wound up with an easy play with this clean-cut guy. We bought way too much coke with all his money and with too much time on his hands, I listened to him rant.

When he went into the bathroom to shower, I took off, she giggled and said, "So let's get high!" She opened her little purse she was carrying and placed its contents on the table. As we smoked in excess over the next few hours, I had another near-death seizure which completely freaked Teresa out. She called 911 and told them she had found me that way. When they arrived at the Seaside Motel, Teresa frantically waves them to room number #10 at the very back corner of the complex.

They went into the room and found me on the floor out cold. They started their routine with one on either side of me while on their knees and popped open their kit; they strapped the blood pressure cuff around my arm and away they went. They frantically searched for any trace of a pulse or the sound of breathing coming from my nearly lifeless body as I was lying on the grimy carpet.

"Damn, let's see if we can bring her back from this." It was the third meeting of five between a medic named Charles and me. Also in the room was my cop friend there in Seaside, and he too quietly said some prayers. The medics worked at bringing me out of my latest delirium.

I could hear some voices saying, "Tiff is a good girl, and she could beat this." Repeatedly, they coaxed me to come back to them until I slowly opened my eyes. Looking up at them, I felt shame and embarrassment that I hadn't felt in a very long time; I realized this event was somehow different. I felt bad I had brought them here to me once again. After stabilizing me, the EMTs asked Teresa if she was going to be able to let anyone know I was okay. Tee told them, yes, and she would stay with me. After a few minutes, my head cleared a little, and I told Tee to fix me up so I could get straight.

I took a big hit, and I leveled out. Teresa still shaking because she had heard a little about my affliction, my seizures, but had never witnessed one. I asked her to stay for a little while and tell me about some of the other adventures she had over the years. Worried about me, she gladly stayed and started entertaining me with her stories.

"How about the night I was riding along with some john, and I realize we're getting out into the desolate area west of the city. So, I asked him where we are going, and I wanted him to turn the car around. Before I knew it, he told me to get out of the car. We were miles from anywhere, and I had to walk all the way back to the outskirts of Seaside before anyone picked me up. The asshole just really pissed me off; I bet he did it just to have a big laugh with his pals, or he was some new pimp trying to get his girl some work since I wouldn't be there to compete with her."

While I was still resting, Teresa told me another story to entertain me. "Then, there was that crazy guy who, one afternoon while I was in his room, sprayed me down with a can of lighter fluid and was going to burn me to death because he said, that's what I really wanted. The fact was that he wanted to own me, and that wasn't happening. Just so I could escape, I told him I didn't want to be his wife but someone would soon love him. I had to convince him that dying was not what I wanted that day. Guess there was a glimmer of hope inside me somewhere hiding and quietly begging to come out. He finally let me go shower off the lighter fluid and sent me on my way. So much evil in the world and Satan just seems to be gaining ground," said Teresa.

Nearing daybreak Teresa told me goodbye and left believing I would be alright after I got a little sleep.

Those are just some of the real dangers that are part of life on the street. Sociopaths all around; narcissistic and sadistic personalities that we had to interact with daily. See by now me and others out here have been through more horror than what the world believes could possibly go on. When the news reports a hooker found dead in a back alley of the local hood, people might give it thirty seconds of recognition before going back to whatever they had been doing. The hookers are throwaway people, right? Who cares about them anyway? They deserve what they get for living that way down there in the streets. This is the general reaction of many. Except, we don't deserve it, but rarely do we really know how to recover from it.

Other stories and dangers from the streets included things way too ugly to share. There was always the risk of being jumped by those even less fortunate than Teresa and me. Homeless drug addicts living in despair and poverty who sadly can only steal or hurt others to get high. In every major city in the world, lonely people who have been torn apart by life and addiction and unable to function in society are all too common anymore and are too plentiful in every major city or small town in the world. The number continues to grow daily. Why? Greed mostly.

I was grateful for Kevin's so-called protection, but today, I knew who was really protecting and saving my life for all those years.

On a slow Monday a few days after my last seizure, Teresa met me at my place to chat, watch some T.V., and get high. I told Teresa about the attempted robbery I had experienced when I first came out to the streets. After an hour of watching T.V., Teresa wanted to do another hit and chill for a while longer. As the rush settled down, Tee told me another crazy story.

She began by saying, "One sunny afternoon, as I crossed through an empty field, I saw Mac coming towards me. He walked up on me and grabbed me by the throat in a choke-hold, nearly killing me. He stole the drugs I had just bought and left me for dead. He was supposed to be my friend, so I was caught off guard and in complete shock. Between the hot sun beating down on me and the adrenaline rush brought on as I tried to fight him, I completely passed out. Mac left me in the sand for I don't know how long, and when I woke, I realized even friends out here, were enemies. I said to her, "No way not Mac; I always thought he was cool."

Teresa asked me if I heard of the guy that likes to be called "Mark in the Dark?" This guy liked it pitch dark in the room while he did what he did to the girls that were brought to him. I told Teresa, "I heard about him, and I had told Kevin I wasn't going back there. Kevin took me out there last week. Yes, he is very weird and I guess he didn't like me because he told me to just take my money and go, leave, walk; that he wasn't taking me back. Grateful I wasn't hurt; I trusted my instincts that it was not going to end well whatever was coming my way. I found my way out and a ride back to the mainland. Sometimes just being lucky to escape was all you could hope for and to be glad to have walked away unhurt. Besides, I say, "I want to be able to see what's coming at me."

"Yeah, I know what you mean girl," Teresa replied. I began another story. "Oh damn! I got a good one for you Tee. About six or eight months ago, I got in this guy's car. I was so high and barely paying attention as I climbed in before I realized I was trapped. I was worried about what he wanted to do to me. You know that feeling you get when you feel like you are trapped? So, I plotted out my next move as I talked to him, telling him we should park over by the store, out back where no one would see; but, he kept driving. I realized the inside handle was removed from the door to trap his victims, and I asked him again to pull over. He ignored me as he was slowing down for the light, I reached my arm outside the window and grabbed the door handle. I opened the door as the car veered for a left turn, and I jumped, rolling out onto the road."

I almost didn't believe it myself as I said it; from this moving vehicle to save my life, it was the craziest thing yet I have had to do. I thanked God that no other car was on the road at that moment. I never felt the bone in my hand break from trying to brace myself as I hit the pavement." Teresa looked at me and said, "Oh, that is why you always seem to be rubbing your wrist."

Teresa looks at me and shakes her head. I know she has had, her fair share of near-death escapes and felt blessed to be alive to talk about them. God really did look out for us. "Listen, Tiff," Teresa says, "I gotta go; Kevin will be looking for us soon, and I gotta get some paper."

"Yeah me too, I say, I'll talk to you later," as we part ways.

8

RECOVERY THOUGHTS

The street life was the same day after day, night after night; the faces changed every now and then, but the end result was the same. Sadly, Death in most cases. If I didn't choose recovery, death would come sooner rather than later.

The self-destruction had to stop. I whisper to myself.

I have shared with you many, horrific stories, and I most definitely could share more, but I am hoping, by now, you have realized that this world is not a place you would want to live in. Everyone who descends into this world will leave it one way or the other via recovery or death. So, make the decision not to go down this road because if you think you can get away unscathed, you're wrong. I hope that you see the need to stop now before the destruction is so bad, there is nothing left for you except Recovery or Death.

The change starts inside of you. You ARE important and special, otherwise, God would not have made you in His likeness.

You must make that realization just as I eventually did. Clearly, God is the only reason I am still here and able to share my experiences with you. Why? What was the reason he saw me thru this mystery since childhood? It was like watching from a vantage point high above, looking down on myself, shaking my head in disgust. The enormous dangers I was allowing myself to live in, surrounded by constant unknowns... yes, 'Life' out Here. It should have terrified me to live among people who valued life so little, and I was at first, but it didn't take long for me to be in a state of mind where I was without sensible fear of those that society, in general, had cast out and labeled inferior.

My seizures were growing worse. Days were repeating, and my world was a blur of the same old things over, and over again – serving perverts and their sleazy desires. Life grew darker daily, and with no help in sight, I just moved on through Never-Never Land. Words couldn't describe how I really felt, and if I could have pinpointed something, there wasn't anything I was ready to admit to myself right then. Maybe what was just ahead of me could have been different if I could have remained straight for even a few days to see clearly how big was 'The Trap' – I was being drawn into and how tightly it would bind me.

I was walking out on the Stroll one particular evening; the traffic rolling by slow and steadily, and I was looking to get some dope from my main corner guy, Jermaine. I looked down the block, but I didn't see a soul which usually meant the cops were out in force, unfortunately, I needed to get high. Rounding another corner, I spotted someone standing just out from under the street light, and I thought that my luck had changed, so I quickly stepped up to him and asked for a dime bag. I didn't recognize him as one of the local guys usually out there, so I asked him if he had seen Jermaine.

The new guy shook his head no, then took two bags out of his pocket and handed them to me. I looked at the bags, and I said, "Listen, I can't smoke this yellow shit. I have bad seizures, and I'm not in the mood for one tonight." I handed it back to him and started to walk away when he says, "Oh, I heard about you. You're Big Papa's girl, Shorty Phat. Wait, I got the clean shit right here." We exchanged the money for drugs, and I thanked him and took off to my room to enjoy my new batch of candy. The next morning, as the sun was coming up, I walked back up the block to find the new guy and get some more dope. While we were doing business, two uniformed cops walked up on us, cuff me, read me my rights, and put me in the patrol car. I noticed the guy I bought the two bags from sitting in an unmarked car and realize he was a narc, and I had been stung.

Off to jail, I went... again. I was definitely getting tired of this life.

As I was being admitted to a familiar rehab center, I remember talking with an intake counselor that I had spoken to in the past. According to her, the courts were tired of seeing me come and go through their doors. Nonetheless, they sent me off to do another rehab stint after I completed the short sentence for the drug paraphernalia I was carrying that morning.

One of the first things they tell you upon arriving in rehab is to focus on yourself for the first year. DON'T get into a relationship because nine times out of ten, the relationship usually causes a RELAPSE. This is mostly because either one or both parties are emotionally unstable and are still looking for a fix which now becomes sex. Early recovery needs to be about self-discovery and dealing with painful issues so they don't continue to drag you down. I was telling my counselor about an experience I had after the last time I was here.

While I sat in the office with the counselor that we all were required to see once a week for an hour, I told her about my last time through, and how I had met someone here in rehab. I told her that we both had been doing really well in our recovery program, but I felt really ashamed for some reason. Dr. Smith asks me, "So what happened to you and your friend, and why are you back here?"

"Well, we started a sexual relationship too soon in early recovery and thought we were in love. Fresh out of rehab, we were both working and thought we should get married, believing we had beat the demon for the last time. We even went through all the protocol to get his little girl back from CPS who had taken her after her drug addict mother left her in the hospital days after she was born." Dr. Smith then asks, "So what happened? Sounds like everything was going well."

Shaking my head, I told her, "Matt relapsed the day after we had gotten his daughter back which was only a week after we had moved into our new apartment. Worse than that, he got arrested for buying drugs and went back to prison. So, I had to turn his little girl back over to Child Protective Services, and it just broke my heart Doc."

Dr. Smith smiled weakly, and said, "Well, hopefully, she is doing good and thriving in the home they placed her."

"Yeah, I hope so too. Little Rainey was so sweet, my own kids had embraced her like their own family; they were devastated by this whole thing, too."

Thirty days later I was out of Rehab and found a ride back to my same ol' playground. I hit the stroll to look for Teresa so I could tell her about the sting I got caught in that fateful night. She tells me, "You have to know when you are too screwed up to be out on the Stroll, sweetheart. They are some crazy sons of bitches out there, and Tiff, you can't trust not one of them. If they big or little or any color they might be, they can hurt you quickly and badly. But you got to take some chances or you ain't gonna make no money," she said sternly. "You pick the right guys, and you do the right things with that big smile, and tell them you want them to come back cause they are really special. Well, you might make a place for yourself down here and make that money just roll in cause you still got the body and the looks honey. Do you understand what I'm saying girl?" she asked with a wide knowing grin on her face.

Teresa was not just some black girl working the streets to

support a drug habit or a pimp. She was supporting a family with two kids of her own, plus one of her sisters, with the money she made on the street. She had a long-time boyfriend who was on again, off again, and always promising her that he would find and keep a steady job but never did for long. She said he always gave her money when he came around and stayed for a few weeks or a few months, and he treated her well. However, for her to pay the bills on time, keep the kids from going hungry, and have decent clothes on their backs she did the only work she knew. She had a string of youthful misdemeanors and minor felonies for bad checks and not much of a formal education, but she was smart, and she was down to earth about life on the stroll. Many of her stories about life on the street were actually good lessons on how to survive and make money out here on the Stroll. I was grateful we were friends.

One afternoon, while chillin' under my favorite banyan tree, I thought about a time five years back when I was blessed with some sobriety. Even after relapsing, the Electrical Union had hired me back. I was top drawer and sharp when I was off the drugs, and I was a good worker; I could make it on my own if I gave myself a chance. Being near my children again had helped a lot with the peace of mind I needed. I had found a nice place to live not very far away from them. It seemed things had gotten back on track, and I was happy again. I was working hard and able to visit with my kids which were nice for all of us.

I lost it all again, though, when I went back to those old people, places, and things, just to say "Hi" to the old gang, maybe even show off just how good I was doing. Unfortunately, I just had to test that "just *one last time*" fallacy. How ultimately stupid I really was to believe it, even for a moment, and that's all it took.

I laid there, stared up into the fluffy, white clouds, and thought about the 'Hamster Wheel of Life' I was on, constantly running aimlessly in a circle and getting absolutely nowhere fast. The endless, sleepless days and nights, lonely and sad, hoping to score more drugs to keep that wheel turning in a relentless circle of pitiful torture that further dehumanized me. I knew every relapse resulted from the same thing, putting down my Bible and ignoring that daily discipline to pray to my Higher Power. After being in recovery for over 16 years, in 2018, I can testify with all of my heart that praying every morning for the Lord to give me the strength, courage, guidance, and wisdom to do His will and not mine is why I am still here today. Praying to my Higher Power is how He pulls me up and saves me every day. I need to ask God every morning to help me, so I will love myself, as he loves me, and thank Him every evening for getting me through another day clean and sober.

It was only by forgetting this that I had failed myself. However, in my past, I would pray just to survive that day. After all those years of existing on the streets, it was hard to keep track of time in any linear fashion, but I did the best I could to know what day of the week it was and which year I was currently living in, well, if you could call it living.

This day, I had just scored a big chunk of cash and was looking to score some candy; I was on the other side of Seaside, so I went looking to see if McCoy was in his favorite place. That side of town was not as busy as down near the marina where I normally hung out, but today I was in need of a few laughs just to ease the feelings of drudgery I was having. I liked to hang out with McCoy when he wasn't busy selling; he too was a user but a nice guy and would look forward to getting high with me and having my company for a couple of hours. We stayed out of the heat in the small shack he called home. We laughed about the cops almost catching some john who was trying to pick up Maggi the other night during the sting operation. We talked about when the new girl, Lynette, who was busted that night and showed back up a few days later looking to score; we were thinking that she was probably a cop.

We really busted up laughing when McCoy said, "I was sitting here in my little corner watching the cop cars racing up and down the streets on both sides for about 20 minutes when Mac came running by me. He was followed by this new rookie cop, who obviously already found the donuts box at the cop shop. Anyways, Mac slithered thru that hole in the fence over there while running from the cops, and the rookie couldn't follow through it, as it's barely big enough for a dog." We laughed and got high for a bit longer than McCoy said he needed to get back to work, as did I.

After another long day in the heat, followed by another humid night, the air was stifling, and I was tired and needed a hit. I went around the back of the VFW hall and lit up a big blast when my ears started ringing, and I knew ... what was coming next.

I forced myself to get out from the back of the building as quickly as I could and headed across the empty lot towards the gas station on the corner where I figured somebody would notice me flopping around on the ground like a fish out of water. The very last thing I remembered was looking down at the sand underneath my feet in the dark of the night.

Waking up covered in sweat and sand; the heat of the morning sun was burning my dehydrated skin. My tongue was bitten and swollen from the seizure I apparently had; what I didn't understand was how I ended up all the way across town from where I last remember being by the VFW hall. It was like 4 miles south of where I was now, but then the thought hit me that someone must have moved my body and left me for the cops to find or the coroner's office to pick up. The money I needed to pay my rent was gone; my rent was three days late, and I knew that jerk of a manager wasn't gonna let me in my room until I paid it up, so I was gonna have to find somewhere to go and rest.

My brain was fuzzy, and I needed a drink of water badly. My legs were throbbing from the massive seizure I had but I forced myself to get up. I could barely walk as I stumbled into Raul's little food store, and he just looked at me and said; "Damn, Tiff, you look terrible. Had another one of those fits, didn't ya?" All I could say was 'yes' and I begged him for a bottle of water. He gladly gave me one and asked if I wanted to lie down in the back of the store. I thanked him, but said, no. What I needed was some money fast, so I could get a hit before my entire body locked up for good. An hour later, my mission was complete, and I was blissfully stocked up and on my way to oblivion once more.

Time was ticking away for all of us out here; the cops were tired of responding to calls of overdoses or drug dealers standing on the corners while children tried to play in their yards. People around here were always wondering if today was the day the gang down the road would retaliate and riddle the streets with bullets. These were the everyday things that happened in this area and many others around the world. Kevin and his pals were no exception. The cops started rounding up everyone they could when the new police chief wanted to set an example and remove the corruption that plagued the city of Seaside.

Kevin's abuse of his girls finally caught up with him. Jessica had been shot in the hip while trying to run from him because she had stolen money, and he wasn't having it. She was dumped in a nasty dumpster and left for dead; it's lucky for her someone found her and called 911.

When she recovered from her injuries, angry and betrayed by him again, she had lots to tell the cops.

He faced charges of White Slavery, Drug Trafficking, Extortion, and Racketeering. These were just some of the extreme charges they had against Kevin on that fateful day a couple of years later when he was locked up for life. Off to the Federal Penitentiary, he went, but the show had to go on, and so it shifted to a new set of actors. One of his Lieutenants, Bruce, then stepped in and continued running the show during the time of his absence. He was in charge of quite an enterprise of drugs, girls, and paying off the cops to ensure they looked the other way on most days. Kevin had gone to prison multiple times over the ten years I was on the streets. I would again, end up alone, but his protection remained. I would be responsible for making sure that my basic necessities of life were taken care of, for example, the rent on my little room, my laundry was done weekly, and things like food and sleep.

Can any of this ever change? I asked myself the question

quietly, but I doubted it ever could or things wouldn't still be so distraught in the world.

How do we convince people to stop before it's too late? How do we convince ourselves we can be all that we once believed we could be? How can they see this ugly world and avoid it, after all, they have witnessed as children or young adults fumbling along and trying to figure out life? We lived with people screaming at us from cars driving by, those who judged the people we were. We were blasted steadily by the sheer cause and effect of being labeled. The stigma of words, such as HO! whore and prostitute, felon or druggie.

Though, I didn't care anymore. Between the addiction and loss of focus for my life that I once had and the one I traded it in for, I was surely doomed to die. My only other friends were on the corners and labeled drug dealers and pimps. Is there any way for redemption and change in my life? Only God knew, and He would soon get my attention. I quietly repeat this prayer to myself.

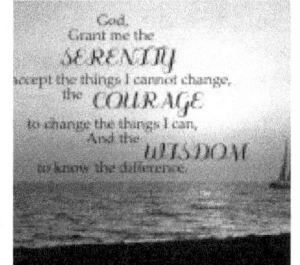 God grant me the *Serenity* to accept. Someone quietly whispers back, "Take my hand and I will walk you through this."

These words finally sank in. I was grateful to see a light at the end of this awful tunnel, even as dim as it was, and God was letting me know there was another way. I finally believed I could make it as long as I just held my faith. This was my – FIRST REAL CRY FOR HELP!

"Please Lord," I cried, I'm so tired of this, and I've made such a mess of everything. Why wasn't I stronger? How does all the brutal evil around me not scare me? Why does getting clean and facing life again terrify me so badly? I know change is incredibly difficult; reliving all the bad things I have done and perceive I have done to others, causes me such fear.

Is it because of my self-destructive need to use? Is this what is causing doubt in me? Yes, could be the only real answer.

Can I live without my drugs? This is the question to many of us falsely believe the answer to be 'No'.

With years of wasted time and age staring back at me in the mirror, I can barely stand to look at myself, but my life is worth finding that joy that has eluded me. It can be found and that reassuring feeling embraces me. God was there to help. I was changing and I could feel it. All I needed to do was put it into action.

THE BIG TRAP, was that one last time, I talked myself into believing that I really had a hold on my recovery and I could do this just once more; I could get '*HIGH*' and stop. LOL!

With a huge pile of drugs ready for me, I gave it one last big bang. I was feeling just a bit nervous, so I left the door unlocked just in case. It was a good thing, too, because somebody sent them to help.

The Seascape Inn was a dumpy, white, two-story, "U" shaped motel with one side facing an empty lot and on the other side, a six-foot, white fence. Decent kind of place for tourists during the season, but the manager will do anything during the slow months to make a buck; so he rents rooms hourly on one side of the building or in the back. A couple of local pimps keep him "satisfied" so the hookers frequent the place, and for a good tip, the guy gives them a good deal and sort of a bodyguard to look out for them.

It was early morning, about 3:00 a.m., the EMTs responded to another call at the Seascape; after hundreds of calls such as this, they were numb to yet another call to this crappy motel. With the door slightly open of the brightly lit room, it didn't surprise them to see there was a body lying on the floor. Opening up the side racks on either side of the unit, they quickly grabbed their emergency medical kits. Once in the room, they could see a white, medium-built, female, in her late twenty's to mid thirty's, unconscious, and completely naked. They opened their kits and knelt down on opposite sides of my body and begun their evaluation of my condition.

"Looks like she might be a party girl or her boyfriend left her for dead," said Charles. "She's pretty bad," Blanchard said as he cinched the Velcro strap of the blood pressure cuff around her upper arm.

"Damn, I know her. She was working at Sullivan's Café the last time I saw her. She OD'd before a couple of doors down around Christmas; Rick and I took her in. I stopped at Sullivan's for dinner after my shift, maybe two or three days before Easter, and there she was standing in front of me smiling and taking my order," Charles said.

"Give her 15 cc's; she's low and slow," Blanchard said affirming the dosage Charles needed to administer to me; he hoped this would revive me to consciousness. He was on my right side applying the stethoscope to my bare chest, over one lung, and then the other listening to the slow, ragged breathing while reading the blood pressure indicator strapped on my arm.

"Where's her pimp when she needs him? I don't think she's gonna make it this time; she's so purple and she's going lower," Blanchard sighed solemnly.

He had done this too many times before in the three years he worked the eleven to seven shift of Firehouse 62's Emergency Response Unit. Hardened by the sights and sounds of Broadway and the Seaside neighborhood that 62 served, their work was gruesome. It was rarely rescuing victims of kitchen fires or the pedestrian accidents that were the regular events that other Firehouses predictably performed day and night. Several of the firehouses and rescue units in the upscale neighborhoods just a few miles away rarely responded to fires, but instead tended to a vast array of injuries involving, strokes, heart attacks, falls in practically every room of a house, from ladders, the roof, or trees in the yard. This was interspersed with removing hands stuck in garbage disposals, cats stuck in trees, or people reporting alligators in their pools or the little ponds behind their homes. He saw those emergencies only on rare occasions, and he much preferred them to the regular cycle of predictable events such as this one.

"Give her five more Charles... she's still dropping," said Blanchard as he placed the stereoscope head under my bare left breast listening to the slowing beat of a human heart he knew was struggling to overcome the effects of a cocaine overload. From the bulging rolled-back eyes and pallid color of my skin and the blood that had flowed and dried around my mouth and on my chest from the deep gashes in my lips and tongue, I had likely endured a severe and prolonged seizure.

He had unfortunately witnessed a few of these almost bizarre spectacles play out before, they had ended like this one when he arrived with the patient comatose and likely fatal beyond his reach to pull them back. My left forearm had a large purple bruise forming and he could safely assume that I was standing when it started. He figured I probably felt dizzy, grabbed the back of the straight-backed wooden chair, started convulsing, and flailed around uncontrollably before finally hitting the edge of the wooden table on my way down to the floor.

Unlike seizures from an allergic reaction, coke and heroin overdoses often produce seizures that induce severe and prolonged muscle convulsions in the arms and legs with enough force to easily break or shatter bones. It would be no surprise to him if my wrist and more than one bone in my right hand were broken judging by the deepening skin discoloration and the odd angles of my thumb and forefinger. He would tend to that evaluation when he got my vitals stable and could bring me back to consciousness before I flat-lined and made other injuries a moot point for the coroner to write up.

"Give her five more, she's still dropping," Blanch stated flatly. Holding a syringe in one hand and a small white-labeled vial in the other, Charles extracted a tiny amount of clear liquid from the vial and transferred it to me with a quick jab of the needle into my upper right arm. He was examining my face and head closely looking for any sign of injury, "No obvious sign of head trauma or neck injury," he said to Blanchard.

"Okay, 5 cc's in and flowing," he said to Blanch as he administered the shot. "Good." Blanchard was holding the stethoscope again over my heart listening for an increase in the beat count from the effects of the shots Charles had given me.

For long moments, there was no change which was good, but he needed more from me before he could safely lift and transport me to the ER. Finally, he could hear there was less time space between the weak beats of my heart, so he took a deep satisfied breath of relief and thought that I just might make it. However, he knew it was way, too soon to predict that I was out of danger, but for the immediate moment, I was at least improving.

"Pump her up again," Blanchard told Charles, "she's popping." With an increased pulse rate, he needed to see a corresponding increase in my blood pressure to know that I was making real progress. Charles pumped the cuff up, and they were both looking at the dial intently as it beeped and read out at 100 over 60. I was on the way up, finally, and they could prep me for transport.

"Come on girl... the party ain't over yet," Charles said to lighten the tension both he and Blanch felt knowing they likely arrived a few minutes ahead of me being a fatality. With vitals so low and still going down the survival potential was slim at best.

In his ten-year career, Charles had seen only a few make it back after an episodic drug seizure this severe. Usually, those victims were bigger and heavier than me with a lot more blood flowing through their veins, and they had faster hearts that were used to higher blood pressure that could withstand an overdose jolt. To him, I was a small girl, not even five four and a hundred and twenty pounds in my clothes and shoes, so he thought that I might not be tough enough today to defy the reapers snare.

His hardened combat medic attitude kept him from ever getting emotional when treating any accident victim, but today when he knelt over me, he didn't think I looked like I should be anywhere near this place doing any of this stuff, and he felt a strange twinge of sorrow. A kind of sadness that says this doesn't need to happen today, not here, not now. The magic medicine from his kit can stop my body from going cold and he hoped I would stop the drift away journey I was taking. Beneath his hard emotional armor was a devout Christian belief system, who believed in God and Satan, good and bad, and right and wrong. He believed that good people and not-so-good people, the right choices, and bad choices were the ethereal boundaries of life and for his work as a medic.

The nude woman on the floor was guilty of making some bad choices and maybe wasn't strong enough today to overcome the hard consequences of them. He took a deep breath, held it for a moment, and silently repeated in his head, as he had thousands of times since his father knelt with him beside the bed when he was a young boy, and prayed, "I pray my soul the Lord to keep."

Charles toggles the talk button twice on his radio and waited for the answering beeps and a voice on the other end at St. Mary's. The responding beep in the radio was followed by a calm male voice acknowledging, "St. Mary's Emergency Room, go ahead.

"Firehouse 62 EMU. We have an unidentified white female, unconscious, possible drug seizure, no major trauma visible, no bleeding, vitals stable, but low, and ready to transport," Charles reeled off the data to notify the ER unit director and waited for confirmation to transport me to their ER. "62, transport when ready," was the response from St. Mary's. "I'll get the wagon," Charles said and went out the door to pull the wheeled gurney out of the van and into the room to take me to the ER.

Blanchard looked up because he sensed the presence of someone standing in the doorway. A small, balding man in a red polo shirt with the Seascape Inn logo stenciled on it was peering into the room, "She dead?" Blanch looked hard at him wondering if he knew the identity of the woman on the floor and why she was in this room naked and unconscious. "No, she isn't, but she is not doing too well. Do you know her? Know who she is?" Blanch asked. He assumed this guy was the manager or at least worked there. "Well no, not exactly. Many people come and go; all I do is sign them in if it's my shift. I don't remember her. I don't remember her checking in." Blanchard knew he was lying but wasn't going to push.

He needed to get up and moving toward the ER, and the small talk with this guy would yield nothing valuable. He stood up, and on a hunch, he pulled open the drawer of the big table that held the TV. Inside of it, there was a small, gray clutch pocketbook just the right size and shape for a woman to carry. He opened it and could see in one of the little pockets was the top edge of a Florida driver's license, so he pulled it out of the wallet. He was looking at the smiling face of Tiffany Rose Baker, 32 years old when Charles came through the door with the gurney.

Blanchard glanced up at Charles and held the driver's license out for him to see, "This, your girl? Tiffany Baker," he asked. "Yep, that's her alright," he said remembering me more like the happy, smiling face at the restaurant on a better day for me. It struck him as sad that so many of the smart ones still wind up on the streets when they shouldn't. The ones like this one with good looks and nice personalities that should be home tucking the kids into bed in a nice neighborhood somewhere instead of a seedy motel turning tricks with strangers.

They lifted my limp body onto the stretcher and wheeled me out of the room and into the van; they sped away lights and sirens clearing their path to St. Mary's. A ten-minute ride was a long journey when a life is hanging in the balance, but I was fortunate this night because I was still stable when they rolled me through the big, double doors of the ER.

Blanch and Charles handed me off to the ER staff, knowing they had done what they could, though my fate was still uncertain. They each filled out the necessary paperwork and signed the logs, exchanged a few cursory hello and goodbye's to familiar faces, and left Tiffany Rose Baker to mend in the hands of those assigned the task of healing. They climbed back into the van and drove back onto the front-lines of the social battlefield one more time with the same questions. Had they pulled her back from the fatal darkness tonight? Would she wake up tomorrow and remember who she was? Would all the parts inside her body still work right? They could only hope.

I did wake from the seizure knowing who I was. The ER doctor and a couple of nurses followed their well-proven checklist, of required protocol and pumped me full of fluids, stabilized me, and asked the all too familiar questions. Did I know my name? Did I know where I was and why? Could I count backward from ten? Did I have someplace to go.

Countless people from the streets, including myself, had put them through this scenario too many times. Before the sun came up, they gave me a clipboard and a pen, told me to sign the discharge paperwork, stood me on my feet, and a nurse walked with me back to the double doors I had passed through only a few hours before. They wished me good luck. What else could they do?

9

THE LONG ROAD BACK

Returning to the motel, I found the manager who did know me very well and the other girls who frequented his motel. I asked him if he had already cleared out my room, and if so, where was the stuff I left in it? He assured me nothing had been touched, and he was glad that I was okay. I went to my room, took a long hot shower, changed clothes, and found my way across town to the stroll. I thought about the cop in the room with the EMTs last night who I was certain knew I had a warrant for leaving the rehab. Why didn't he take me in? Maybe after seeing me on the floor barely alive figured it didn't really make sense to follow me to the hospital and wait to see if I lived through it to arrest me. I'm sure he had more serious matters to deal with than a rehab runaway hooker last night. Maybe he too knew something that I didn't.

I made my way over to the Stroll to do what I had to do while asking myself all the way there, why I hadn't stopped after that last time. Why did I relapse yet again?

Just one more time and that is it, I said to myself. I can do it this time; I know I can.

> *I was clearly out of my mind !!!!!!*

In less than ten minutes, with a steady flow of cars passing, I caught the eye of the guy in a silver sedan, and he pulled to the curb. I walked over, leaned in through the open window, and said I had what he wanted if he was interested. I didn't figure him for an undercover, but he was. In just a few seconds the marked cruiser pulled up, and off to jail I went with the outstanding drug charge warrant the basis for the arrest.

This was my 'LAST TRIP' to Jail. I was set to do a year because of my past choices, and I repeated aloud to myself, "My forties are not going to have me out there hustling any longer "I'm done!"

I resolved to let go of the past sins that were brought on by too much emotional baggage in my lifetime of abuse, to let God take the pain, and I trusted Him to make a way in my life.

I still read from the same tattered Bible.

Knowing that if I miss even ONE day of not speaking to God or asking for that daily direction, even all these years later, my day just doesn't go right. This Bible was a gift from someone very special to me; with the pages wore and torn from the binding and taped back in place, this book has been well-loved and cared for. Just as I have received the same love and care from God over these years as I worked at putting my torn life back together. God carefully taping those ripped-out pages back together, building me into a new person, whole and beautiful, a new soul set to emerge into the world. You too can also have this Love; all you have to do is ask God or your Higher Power, have Faith in yourself, and believe that you deserve this love. Trust that you have the power to change your life. God's love is always with you; all you have to do is search it out, and you will find it.

All those years I spent going to jail for drugs, guns, prostitution, and trespassing, I was always aware and reminded that the Lord was present in my life. Although, I just didn't take the time to search for the answers I needed to succeed. Now, I was ready for the work that it would take. After getting booked into jail those many times before, and being placed in the jailhouse rehab program for however long my sentence was that time, then being transported to an inpatient facility afterward for another 30 days, I would relapse. Not this time!

The intake guard sent me to Sister Ann's program hoping it would help. Finally, I realized that change was mandatory in my life, right now, at this time and place. I had been blessed in so many ways up to this point, now it was either recognize the Lord standing there trying to help or give into Death. Sister Ann was a true Saint; there is no other label, title, or word you could give this woman of God. She was a sweet and caring, God-fearing woman who only wanted to help us realize our true potential. Sister Ann created this recovery program intending to help those who were looking to help themselves.

Nevertheless, this was still jail. Unfortunately, jail is where society just dumps us rejects, druggies, and criminals because it is easier to house us there than to help us. More jails exist in the USA than do medical facilities to help those suffering. The bigger problem truly is we have to want to help ourselves. Without that there is no escape from the malady which haunts us day and night. If you are given a chance that doesn't come often or easily, you should take it; utilize it, and change your world. They or Society, doesn't give us but one chance, usually, so please think of all the good you can have if you walk thru your own fear and into your new life. This was something I was finally willing to do.

The Christian Life Skills Drug Program

Exhausted this last time, I showed up in Sister Ann's dorm with ten years of broken bones, seizures, rapes, beatings, drug overdoses, jail stays, rehab, and recovery attempts. Something had to give, and I was ready to try something new, and make it work. I was going to give 100% of myself to this new life and person desperately trying to emerge. The 12-week program was full of direction, guidance, wisdom, and faith all of which I needed in order to get from here to where I wanted to go in the outside world.

Finally, I gave up my will to follow God's will, and I was ready for the biggest challenge of my life. Armed with my Higher Power, Faith, and the Will to find my way back, my road traveled was full of bumps, twists, turns, and despair, but also so much Hope and Prayer for the Lord to watch my precious loved ones and me. As I prayed, that one day I would be part of their world again, happy, healthy, and enjoying the serenity promised by living a drug-free life.

The <u>**LONG ROAD BACK**</u> ... was going to be much longer than the ugly one I took to get to the dark side. I had a lifetime of pain, abuse, and torture, and I truly wanted to be free.

I had become an empty shell after slowly being sucked into a dark and ugly world I once lived in with pain of monstrous proportions, but I was ready to leave it behind and find a new life, a life reshaped into something special.

I wanted to be a woman I was proud of and have a life worth living. I was like the seedling pushing out of the earth, as my roots took hold and strengthen... I needed to push myself up and out of the dark dirt, so I could grow and become the beautiful flower that God knows I am.

With the past no longer drowned out by the drugs, I was terrified and wondered if I could actually do it this time, yes I surrendered. I was ready to give 100% and make it work, and though it wasn't the first time I tried to mend this fence, everyone, including myself, was tired of all the broken promises.

Now, almost 40 years old, the toughest fight of my life was standing before me. I knew it was going to take a lot of strength to walk this new road. Life had been cruel, yes, but I was not going to let it be a crutch any longer and I had to admit some of it was my fault.

Much of the information that would be presented to me was not new, but the manner in which it would be shared with me this time would impact me. Perhaps hearing the information from people who had actually lived the same life as I had made me realize that I, too, could change my life for the better. Even though I've always known I was not, literally, the only person that lived on the streets, I felt I was all alone. This is a trap our minds fall into because we are afraid we are too far gone or believe we cannot be helped. So, hearing the success stories of others gave me hope. I never tried to share it with anyone or let go of the pain, and this held me down for too long. Not any longer because now I was ready with 100% determination that I wanted to take back my life that was indeed stolen from me.

Why hadn't the various treatments over the years not worked? I couldn't dwell on that question any longer. Today, I was ready for my soul, my world, and all of my being to be transformed. Sister Ann came in daily to pray with us, and maybe that is why I continue this discipline to this day. We had finished breakfast, cleaned up the dorm, and readied ourselves for Sister Ann and our daily prayers.

"Good morning ladies. I hope you all are well today. Does anyone have a special prayer request before I begin?" she asks as she walks into the dorm. With no hands raised or requests made, she carries on with the Morning Prayer. We prayed the Our Father and asked the Lord to bless us with his strength, courage, and guidance to do his will in our lives.

Then, Sister Ann said, "Prayer does not give you Spiritual power. Prayer aligns your life with God so that He chooses to demonstrate His power through you. The purpose of prayer is not to convince God to change your circumstances, but to prepare you to be involved in God's activity." She was silent for a moment to allow us to ponder deeply what this meant. She then looked around the room and told everyone the assignments we were to complete for the day and left us to our work.

The Christian Life Skills program was 12-weeks to completion and although my sentence was halfway done, all I wanted was out of jail and a chance at a fresh start in recovery. I had never really looked forward to recovery before, but of course, I didn't have the desire to make it work. One thing that I learned during all these years behind bars was the procedures of jailhouse law, and I was going to put that knowledge to good use. I asked one of the guards, Ms. Wilson, that seemed like she actually cared about us, for the forms I would need to fill out in order to file a petition directly to the Judge requesting an early release and court date to plead my case. As the days crawled by waiting to hear from the courts, I focused on Prayer and personal change by learning the life skills of this program, along with the classes in Anger Management, Parenting, and AA/ NA 12-Steps. My new spirituality and self-help I was doing, was the therapeutic work that truly set my new life in motion. There was nothing I didn't do to work daily at my new life; nothing was going to stop me any longer from having the life I deserved.

Those days of self-doubt, or was it laziness when I told myself that I couldn't ever get out or how I wouldn't be able to beat the cravings of my drug; these lies were now replaced with words of encouragement to myself. Self-empowerment was growing in me, I reminded myself daily I was a good person.

During those 3 months, I earned all the certificates I needed in order to complete the program. A real sense of accomplishment and pride was steadily filling me. Unlike rehab programs on the outside, Sister Ann's program centered on accountability. It was an integral part of the program, and we had to participate if we wanted to achieve recovery. Since it was a voluntary program if you were not trying, you were not staying.

Also during this last incarceration, as I worked through all my issues that needed attention and dealt with the drama of all these women locked up together, I did what I could to share the hope that was now growing in me. The switch for the light at the end of the tunnel was finally within my reach.

My favorite part of the program was when the NA and AA speakers would come in and talk with us. As they told us their own war stories, so to speak, and accomplishments, I began to feel a new desire for the recovery life growing in me. Becca was one of the regular speakers that came out to see us; her stories inspired me because the world she had escaped from was so much like my own. She was always reminding us, "Girls, you have the power inside yourselves. Dig deep and find that one thing that still holds you down, then talk about it with your peers. It will help; I promise." She told us to keep a journal if we weren't comfortable talking with a peer. Even by writing it down, we were releasing the power it had over us. We were taking control. I liked her thinking, and I began writing down my dark secrets, and as she promised, they became less haunting. Ms. Wilson called me to the guard desk out in the main area of the dorm one afternoon, and said, "Looks like you get to go see the Judge about your furlough. Good work, girl." I just smiled and thanked her. The furlough was to deal with my disability paperwork. Yes, by now I had already previously tried to get my disability. I started the process when I was straight, but I stumbled and relapsed before I had the chance to go back to the social security office. Going to jail forfeits the application and you have to wait one year before you can reapply.

This was another hamster wheel of its own, but rules are rules, and those were the rules for social security.

When I had finally received this approval, I had a lot of apprehensions. I was trying not to miss another appointment, as this was my second attempt to apply for help. Unfortunately, they denied me and said that I could get a lawyer and try again. This was, of course, because I was still in jail and all benefits or applications become inactive or void. Depending on where in the process your case has fallen with social security.

This really was a true test of my Faith and a crossroad in my recovery or continued addiction. I was so frustrated and thinking all kinds of uneasy thoughts, but something kept telling me to 'hold on'. I was finally on that right road now and wanted to stay; this new place of serenity and calm, happiness that didn't come from some drug or drink which was a new concept for me, was embracing me.

I thought about relapsing that day while I was on furlough just for a brief moment, after leaving the social security office. Totally pissed off, thinking, "Well I could run again, and when they catch me, I'll deal with it then." However, something had hold of me this time and was giving me new strength. I felt that if I went back to jail and finished my time, God would take care of my future. He did and I've taken it one day at a time, His way, ever since.

You can also find that strength in yourself and search out a better life, too. Relinquishing control over my life and trusting in the Lord to carry me through has given me a feeling of absolute peace. A belief that it will work out if I just hold on today.

So, back to the jailhouse, I went, and needless to say, I was very discouraged about my disability monies. I had hoped that money would enable me a fresh start in my new life, but I wasn't going to let it defeat me. Something would work out for me!

I was also very proud of myself that I hadn't relapsed that day because I had one other place to go before I returned to the jail. I actually had gone into the hood to retrieve pictures of my kids and some clothes that were at Kevin's place, if the other girls hadn't already taken what might still fit me. I knocked on the door and waited. Kevin couldn't believe I was at the door and stood there just looking at me. This big brute of a man who loved me with the capacity available to him during those years I spent on the street under his watchful eyes, was amazed and glad to see me. Kevin asked me, "How did you get out? I thought you had another six months to go."

I told him why I was out on furlough, and how they let me go to the social security office to check on my disability case. He just stared at me incredulously. I asked where my stuff was because I wanted the pictures of my kids that were there. I told him I was going back to the jailhouse and shaking inside the whole time. Not because I was scared of him, but because I was scared of myself and whether I could leave there without making that crucial mistake.

"Right now, please Kevin. If you ever cared about me, please just let me go."

He brought me over to where he had my things, and I quickly grabbed the pictures. Kevin gave me a kiss on the cheek, and said, "Tiff, you know I love you, and I hope you know that I'm proud of you for finally getting out." My heart was pounding so fast and my hands were shaking and sweaty. I was clenching them so tight my fingernails had dug marks in my palms. I don't recommend what I did to anyone. Don't ever put yourself in this situation when you are still new to recovery. Nevertheless, I wanted those pictures to help keep me focused on what I finally was ready to face.

Kevin walked me back to the door, gave me a hug, and said, "Here Tiff," he handed me twenty dollars, "get something to eat before you go back to the jailhouse."

After I made it back to West Palm Beach, I tried eating, but it just wasn't working as my stomach felt sick from going into the lion's den, so to speak. I still had a few hours to kill before I was due back, so I spent those hours just walking around, window shopping, and reflecting on the choice of the moment. Finally, after walking back through the door at the front of the jail's intake area, a guard fingerprinted me and booked me back in. I knew that I was ready to complete the punishment and rehab; it's funny because we don't think about this happening during those times when we are getting high. When I transferred back to the jailhouse rehab program, I sat down to tell my only friend, Sally Mae, all about my adventure. We could relate to each other because our stories were so similar; the pain we felt was so alike; it was as if we were sisters. On some level, our bond helped both of us deal with the reality of what we were facing. Maybe one day we would share our stories with someone else and help inspire them to fight for their lives in recovery.

I guess you could say it was like paying it forward; to be a glimmer of hope for the lost by telling my story, and sharing tears with them would be a "coming full circle" kind of feeling. Just as I found hope and inspiration from a former cellmate, Toni. On her last day here, she had given me a book containing stories of Jesus and his message; it was a book that was tattered and torn and was a gift to her from another recovering addict wanting to help. Inspiring each other was all we had inside this jail. We looked forward to those who would come to share their time with us and help us better our lives by teaching faith and hope for another day. Sally Mae was a young heroin addict with her own very sad story and began hooking so she too, could leave behind her ugly world. She was sexually and emotionally abused at a very young age by her father, so she used drugs to lessen the pain; a pain that ran very deep. Sally Mae and I were close; we studied together, discussed the Bible, and because we were still in jail, we watched each other's back.

One particular afternoon, Sally Mae sat down on my bunk and asked if we could talk; of course, I said yes. She started crying as she said, "I can't stop thinking about all those johns, and the disgusting things they wanted. I never want to relive any of that again. I can finally feel again now that the detox symptoms faded and the cravings subsided, and I feel I can do this now. I believe I can stay clean after I get out of here." She acknowledged that we were both in here for the long haul; as she was looking at almost a year herself. Sally Mae then said, "Tiffy, I'm glad I was put in here. I was so close to death from the infection in my arm." I gave her a hug and told her she would be okay, and that God would help her find her way.

I liked being in this particular program because it gave me opportunities to learn about things I had missed over practically, a lifetime. Between all the program teachers, NA and AA speakers, and spiritual Preachers, there was always something to do and learn. This gave anyone who actually wanted the knowledge and had the courage to grow – plenty of it. The program required you to stay up during the day as if you had a real job, so it helped regulate your body clock to the normal 9 A.M.–5 P.M. type of work routine; this helped you prepare for the reality of what was expected of you when you were released into the real world.

The 'Yard' was where we got our one hour a day of sun and the chance to socialize with one another, of course, that is if the guards felt like taking us out. During this brief time, we were able to breathe some fresh air and feel almost human as the sun hit our faces; it felt so good even if we were herded outside like cattle.

Today as I was happily walking the yard by myself and reflecting on my new life and the hopes of leaving these barbed wire fences very soon. A new girl, LaQuisha, came up to me and tried to cause a fight. At this point in rehab, I had found my strength through recovery and had become a strong and serene girl who was growing daily. I had re-trained myself during one of my required classes in how to react to things that not so long ago, would have angered me, guess that class was working too. I had found a way to bring about a true calm feeling, a serene existence, instead of the hard and fast reactions I once lived.

The Serenity Prayer was a part of my daily life. God and the program were all I focused on and lived so that I would never come back to this world again. I saw what God was trying to show me and I could now hear his loving voice ever so quietly. "You can do this Tiff and live a new life." As I watched her and listened to her words trying to provoke me, I prayed, "Lord give me strength."

While this girl is all up in my face saying, "So you're from that God-lover rehab program? Give me a break and your ring, bitch." This really made me wonder what Satan was trying to prove or was he testing me? Ready to stand my ground and face what surely would not be the last battle where I would have to stand up for myself and my recovery, I looked her in the face, and said, "No hun, I don't think it'll fit your finger."

I had bought myself a birthday present one year out there on the streets, a gift to myself, a small reminder that I was important. It was a gold heart-shaped pinky ring. The intake guard couldn't get it off my hand the day I was booked into the jail system and I wasn't giving it up now. I still wear that ring today, just as a reminder of a life once lived and my escape from hell, a warrior absolutely! Oh and this aggression towards me... was not going to end well for LaQuisha. With a knowing look in my eye and the Serenity Prayer on my tongue, I said, "Listen, I know you're scared, and you think this will make you look tough, but please let me show you another way. God can Help! Why don't you join the program?

LaQuisha laughed at me and started to walk away when Ms. Grant, today's guard walked by and asked if everything was okay? A large crowd had gathered to see a fight, so she had come over to check it out. I replied, "Oh yes, we're good. We were just speaking about God and Sister Ann's program. That it's a good program with a lot of informative classes to learn new stuff." Ms. Grant looked at us both and then told LaQuisha to go to the other side of the yard. I may not have gotten her to see the power of God or join the program, but I did get her to see the power of God and his presence which was now apparent in my life.

Sister Ann's program was taking hold, and I was so grateful for this one last chance to prove to myself that I could enjoy a life not consumed by drugs and torture. I was ready to fight for it at all costs. While I was sitting in class one day a guard came to tell me I was being transferred from the program to the Trustee Dorm for work detail. They moved me from the program I so desperately wanted to be successful in. It had to be a test from God to see if I really believed and was really committed to my recovery. Was my faith strong enough for the road that lay ahead; I had to look deep in my heart for the answer.

I was going to have to answer these hard questions or fail at my recovery again. Why?

Why did I hide from the world all those years? Why didn't I try harder?

With all the broken bones from the years gone by, I was in no shape to work in this kitchen. In here a production line of inmates were filling trays of food for the entire jailhouse population, stacking trays, and filling crates of milk or coolers of Kool-Aid for transport to the separate dorms. It was not fun, and it was also dangerous for me because the broken bones from my collarbone were left jagged and were separated by three inches of missing bone. I could easily puncture my lung if I fell on my shoulder slipping on this wet floor. I needed to get out of this kitchen, and I would use my previous injuries as my ticket out and back to the program I desperately needed.

I sent a request to the warden that I am returned to the dorm they had taken me from due to my prior injuries that were well documented in my intake records. I also asked for the name of the person who was responsible for my new placement because I wanted my children to know who they should file a lawsuit against if I should accidentally fall while working. It was the next day that they transferred me back to the program dorm, and I understood that I passed God's test.

The program was filled with plenty of young girls who fell off track in their own lives. For example, there was Heather, who during her teens was prescribed Percocet by her doctor for a condition she suffered during her menstrual cycle. Sharing during group one day Heather told us, "I found as the years went by I needed harder drugs to stop the pain because my body was building up a tolerance to the drugs that were not as strong. Now, I'm lost in this world and trapped because of the system's negligence and pill-pushing doctors just trying to get rich. I was stealing so I could buy off the streets, and well, here I am. I'm left with just a bit of Hope of finding a way out of 'the life'. Just as Tiffany had all those other times too." I was shocked she had used me as a reference, and I went over to Heather, gave her a reassuring hug, and told her it would be okay. We all were wondering to ourselves what it was going to take to put our lives back together, to return home to our children left crying because they miss their mommy.

I had just about given up hope to see the judge when finally word came that Judge Brown had allowed me a hearing to present my case for an early release. I had spent these last few weeks getting together all the certificates I earned for completing each of the classes that were part of the program, and I enjoyed a real sense of accomplishment. I could feel the confidence that was growing in me. I felt a huge weight lift from my shoulders and the ugliness of the old world being erased.

There was a new hope that was shining a bit brighter each day with a sense of peace inside me I had never felt before in recovery. The spirit inside of me wanted to change, but I had to earn it, and hard work was mandatory for change to take place. It is not going to come knocking on my door; I would have to go make it happen.

NO ONE was giving me a free ride.

The spirit of a new life waiting to be reborn into the woman I always was meant to be – a caring, loving, and God-fearing person. I was happy and smiling with a feeling that was foreign to me, but so very good at the same time. JESUS had never left me.

Now, I was going to have to be very committed to the change in my life if I was to succeed this time, and I knew that half-measures never ever worked before. The one thing that was so, so very clear to me now was the need to express my gratitude every day for the blessings in my life. So I pray, "Thank you, Lord, for all you do each day in my life."

Ms. Wilson called out the names of those who were to be ready for court; I was barely able to eat and paced with my folder in hand. At 6 a.m., I was shackled at the waist and ankles; this was a result of that gun felony way back when. I waited to be loaded on a bus with the other girls that were also on their way to court to find out their fate from the justice system and what their bad choices were now going to cost them. As I shuffled past Ms. Wilson, she gave me a little wink of approval, and quietly said, "Good Luck." I sat quietly on the bus practicing in my head what I wanted to say to Judge Brown. This day was finally a reality, and I wanted the Judge to know why I was deserving of an early release after all the drugs and the criminal activities I had participated in over the years. This day was going to end up being one of the longest and most rewarding days of my life. I could not have been more proud of myself that day December 19th, 2002, as I stepped onto the bus ready to advocate for my new chance in life.

God was going to make me reflect all day on the years gone by to know what truth was in my heart, and He was going to help me see that which I had been missing all these years. Patience was definitely something I lacked back then and long into my recovery. This tattered Bible is my daily discipline of prayer and truth.

When the morning sessions ended the other girls had gone and come from their appointed courtrooms, here I sat cold, anxious, and still waiting for my trip up the elevator to the courtroom assigned to my case. As I paced back and forth across the small holding cell in the basement of the courthouse, I prayed while the knot in my stomach was growing more painful.

As the guards came to collect the girls that were on their way back to the jailhouse, the guard in charge handed me a bagged lunch, and said, "Sorry, you're going to have to wait for afternoon court." I took the brown lunch bag and looked inside at a squished, peanut butter and jelly sandwich, apple, and an oatmeal cookie, but at least it was lunch I thought. I would have to drink water from my hands cupped under the faucet of the sink.

Sad-faced and now very nervous, I prayed aloud as I sat there on the cold metal bench all alone in the dark basement cell. The faded, white, cement block walls of the courthouse cell seemed to close in on me. Knowing that no one would see, I hit my knees and began "Lord, I know I have failed you, myself, and everyone I love in the past. Please, forgive me and allow me another chance to redeem myself; I know that I can do this if only you will continue to guide me. I will spend the rest of my days loving others as you have loved me and helped me love myself."

I lifted myself off the dirty floor and closed my eyes to rest on the cold metal bench; the afternoon passed very slowly. I paced while the afternoon's set of girls also went up and came down from their courtrooms. Finally, it was my turn and up the elevator, I went with a smile in my heart and the anticipation of a fresh start on my mind; I was grateful for this chance to speak with the Judge.

The guards set each of us in the gallery seating area while we awaited our turn with the court-appointed lawyer. Since I had requested the hearing I was not represented by counsel.

When it was my turn, Judge Brown looked at me and asked, "Why are you before this court today, for the record?" I nervously cleared my throat before speaking, "Judge I'm here today to request an early release from jail. I'm in the Christian Recovery Life Skills program at the Stockade, and I have done almost 5 months of my sentence and have completed the recovery program. I am determined to get my life on track and find a better way to live life in a clean and sober manner. I promise to never get in trouble again or use drugs." I meant it this time.

I was ready for the long road I would face and do whatever it took to get there. No stone would be left unturned in my quest to repair all that was broken within myself. As I blankly stared at the Judge my mind drifted off to why I had to do all this time. My membership in the world I once belonged to gave me protection and street cred with the others out there. The corruption within the legal system ran deep and there had been quite a few unanswered charges that had been adjusted to look like they were closed which were completed by an employee at the clerk's office of the county courthouse that I was standing in today. In addition, was the six-month inpatient rehab program I had walked away from eight months earlier. Now that sentence came from my third Felony – Drug possession charge in July 2001 and it carried one year in jail or a 6-month Rehabilitation program to be completed. The first six weeks back in jail, I had visited the courthouse to answer to; misdemeanor charges of solicitation, trespassing, and a few other charges. The courts ran all those charges concurrent with the one-year charge for the felony and for walking out of rehab. The Lord, once again, had blessed me as I could have received a five-year charge for escape because I had left rehab.

As Judge Brown looked at the Prosecutor, he asked, "Well Madam Prosecutor, what do you think?" I was snapped back to the moment by his voice and looked over at the prosecutor. This prosecutor was definitely tired of seeing me in her courtroom, and with all the charges on my rap sheet, plus all the chances I had received over the years, I could tell she held great disdain for me. I didn't think she was willing to help any further, so with a smug look at me and then back at Judge Brown, she said, "Well when the defendant can prove that she has completed all portions of the program, she is "Free to Go!"

My heart jumped with "Joy" and as I smiled inside I felt the glow must have lit up the room, and I let a confident smile appear on my face. I opened the folder in my shaking hands, and I humbly took hold of the Certificates carefully tucked inside, one by one I started pulling them out of the folder. Each certificate for each part of the program was there – Parenting skills, Anger Management, 12-Step Recovery program, Spirituality, and others. I was still smiling inside as I showed them first to the Judge by holding them up and then I handed them to the guard, who then handed them to Judge Brown. He looked at each one and then looked at the Prosecutor. All he could say to me was, "Guess you're going home today. You're free to go.

All the charges were closed, and I returned to the jailhouse that evening waiting for my release back to the outside world. I had no idea how I was going to make this work, but I knew that God would help me figure it out because he was clearly in charge now. I truly did have something to be proud of in myself for having the courage to even write that letter or go into the courtroom and speak up for myself.

Ms. Wilson, the guard, reminded me of these things upon my return to the dorm after court and said she was really proud of me and hoped one day down the road, we would cross paths and talk about how well it all turned out. This would not be the last time I would have to stand up for myself or fight the system for a life I deserved. The world was not going to make this easy for me, but I was not to be defeated any longer.

There was a new life out there for me and I was going to find it.

I was giddy with the joy of a little child. I knew if I could stay straight and take the necessary steps to maintain it, then I would recover and rebuild my life. My plan was now set in motion just waiting for its execution with precision and care. It was one week before Christmas 2002 and I was quite unnerved as to what I was going to do with myself over the holidays. God was talking to me and I was finally ready to listen. I had received a true gift from God! A gift I was not going to waste again it was such a wonderful "Present".

10

CROSSROADS

Being released just before Christmas would have at any other time of my life, brought on a deep depression and extreme use, but this gift from God was overwhelming and not to be disrespected. This day I gave all the glory to God, and I had a real glow beaming from inside as I walked up out of that courthouse. This was going to be the last time I would do so if I had any say in it, and ultimately I did.

After getting back to the jail, I waited five hours for processing out of the system. I had returned from court with such excitement that I immediately stripped my bunk, bagged my few things, and waited. As each hour passed, the clock got closer to midnight, and all the other inmates were whispering, "She's not being released in 5 months, she must be crazy," I overheard. At midnight the jail door slid open with a slow crawl.

I was FREE and ready to keep my promise to God and myself. It was the "Time of Truth." Would I finally do the right thing for my life or fail myself once again?

As the cold December air hit me, the rush of reality did as well.

I looked up at the stars and was never more thankful to see them shining down on me. "I've got nowhere to go, not even a halfway house this time," I heard myself mumbling, "not that I made that work before either." Still mumbling out loud, I said, "I really have to do something new this time because the old way seems to take me right back to where I started which was here."

I looked at my cell phone and hoped it had enough charge for just one call. My hands were cold, and the chilly air was running right through me standing in the dark, cold night in late December. Before I could do anything I needed to get warm or as warm as possible, considering what I had on, which was not very much. Picking up my bag, I took inventory of what it contained. I had a couple of t-shirts, socks, some books and papers from the program, and the file folder that held my precious certificates and the reason for my freedom this night.

Normally, the jailhouse rule is you leave your personal things for those others still inside; it was exactly how I had gotten these few things. However, the old superstition among us was if you leave anything behind you will be back in for it. I was not going back, so I took everything with me, even the hair bands, and it was a good thing too. I layered the shirts over my tank top trying to stay warm; they were dingy jailhouse things, but it was all I had to wear right now. I would buy some new clothes from Goodwill soon enough.

I was scared at the thought of starting over.

Where was I going to go? How was I going to eat? I was armed with the knowledge to pursue a better life, and I believed I had the fortitude to be successful, but standing out there in the cold at midnight, I was a bundle of nerves and goosebumps in the freezing cold weather. I was grateful for another chance and though I knew starting over was hard, my resolve was I would not fail again as I had in the past.

Accountability is foremost, first to yourself than to the people trying to help you. It takes Responsibility on your part to make it work, so search for the help you need and don't be afraid to ask for it. I had set goals so I would be able to find my way out of this mess. On this particular day, my goal was to finish the program, get out of jail and never come back.

Tomorrow's goal and my short-term future; I would stay clean and sober, find work, housing, and transportation, even if it meant walking or having to ride three buses to get to work. I was ready to make that commitment. The basics, such as food, water, and clean clothes, those necessities that most take for granted, I also needed. In addition, since I had not worked in a long time, I was going to have to retrain my old way of thinking and myself. I was going to make it work no matter what it took this time. My life finally seemed to matter again to me.

After getting those t-shirts and socks layered on, my shoes now felt funny, but I was warmer. I picked the phone back up and looked for his number. Kurt had promised months back that he was just a phone call away if I ever needed anything. I was hoping it would be more than just a ride away from the jailhouse.

Kurt had picked me up one night not long after a relapse. He told me that I deserved better than the life I was leading. He really didn't have a clue what I walked away from, but God must have sent Kurt to me that night to tell me, "God can help." Those words stuck with me even though they insulted me at the time, and not because I didn't believe in God, but because I felt too unworthy at the time to trust in Him.

Kurt had given me his number the first night we met and said to call anytime day or night; I hoped he wouldn't regret it now.

It was ringing, oh, Praise God, but after four rings I was just about to hang up the phone when he answered. His husky, familiar voice on the other end said; "Hello? Who is this?"

I was so nervous that I almost hung up the phone. It started to fall out of my hand, but I caught it in mid-air and put the phone back to my ear. "Hello? Is someone there?" I heard him say.

Very softly, I said, "Hi Kurt, It's me, Tiffy. How are you?" after a brief pause I continued, "Listen, I need your help. Sorry, it's so late." I held my breath waiting for his response. With just a bit of confusion in his voice, and understandably so since I had just woke him up at one in the morning, he said, "Tiff? Where have you been? I tried to find you a couple of times!"

I thought to myself and smiled, Kurt had looked for me a few times when I was locked up? No amount of words could express how lucky I felt at that moment to have him there for me, and his voice sounded as though he really did care that I was doing okay. "I was in Jail!" I blurted out when I found my voice again holding back the first tears I felt coming.

I just got released, and I don't want to go back to that life. Please, I have nowhere to go tonight. I want a better life. I do not want to die on the streets. I want out of that world and drug life. Honestly, I'm tired of it all," I told him with pain and sincerity in my voice.

"Can you please help me until I figure out what to do? It's cold out here, and I'm in shorts and I don't have a jacket. I'm lucky this battery is still active. It'll probably die soon. Will you please come to get me? Please, Kurt." I was trembling from the cold.

A million horrible thoughts stirred in me and my blood felt like ice water in my veins. I was in the jailhouse parking lot in the middle of the night and so afraid he would hang up on me, and I couldn't blame him. Kurt said, "It's Midnight! Why in the hell did they let you out in the middle of the night? That's not cool. Sure I'll be there soon. Try to find somewhere to stay warm and hang up to save the battery."

"OK. See you soon and thank you, Kurt." I couldn't believe what I had just heard.

Finding somewhere to stay warm without having to go back inside the jail's visitor area was going to be hard. I wasn't going to set foot back inside, even if I was freezing to death. When I scanned the area around the parking lot perimeter I saw a few trees over by the edge of the parking lot to the east. On the other hand, the cars parked in the lighted parking lot were all lined up in their respected box of space, so I could huddle up against a car to block the cold wind that was blowing.

I thought about the long bridge that ran from the jail to the parking lot; it was my best option because the staircase was thirty steps deep, and the handrail was made into a cement wall and would do a great job of blocking the biggest amount of wind. I ran over there and snuggled up on the steps as close to the wall as I could possibly get, and pulled my knees up to my chest. I thought if I could get them up as close to my body as possible, I just might be able to stay warm. Hope settled in as I sat there pondering what was next in my life.

Kurt, a man I barely knew, was coming to save me from the ugly beast inside that I was ready to get rid of and never to see again. Yet, I really didn't know anything about Kurt or who he was outside of the hour here or there when I was with him on a couple of previous occasions.

As I sat there in the dark, families would walk by on their way to the jail to post a bond to free a loved one from having to be in jail overnight. Many of them were scared parents fearing for their children and wishing they could figure out a way to save them. Forced only by the reality of what life could become as they too stood out here watching and waiting for those being released and watching as the local police brought prisoners in to be booked. This booking area is used as the first step to answer for whatever crime had been committed; this place is a stepping stone and for some a life-ending journey. Those people who would now be monitored day and night under lock and key by the law; it was a stark new reality for all involved.

My choice now was to change and having been given the chance I was taking it. I wanted that chance to live right and enjoy the life I had been blessed with, and "I was going to make it happen no matter what," I would repeat this often. Tonight, even if it meant sleeping in the house of an ex-john.

About an hour had passed, and the night was getting colder as that voice of self-doubt started creeping in. I decided to leave figuring Kurt wasn't really coming. Why would he want to help some junkie whore? I was aimlessly walking across the parking lot thinking about what my next move was going to be. Many people struggle to make connections with people on the outside when leaving jail or rehab, because really by this point, we have burned most of our bridges of support, and I surely had no one to speak of in my life other than those I was trying to get as far away from as possible.

There was no extended family here in Florida, at least not that I knew of because I hadn't called Auntie Hazel in a long time to find out how everyone in Texas had been doing or to tell her...What? How bad I had screwed up my life! Why would anyone in my family want to help me? Those that had tried before had already given what they could to help and to no avail. So, this time it was all on me, and I was going to figure this out on my own. There was something different in me, and I could feel it, a confidence that nothing was going to stop me. I felt a resolve that I was going to look in a mirror one day and be so very proud of where I was and cherish all that it took to get there.

God was giving me one last chance to get it right, and this time I was listening. "This time, God," I said to myself; "I'm going to do it, I promise."

"Please, remake me into the woman I need to be, so I can go on and do what I was supposed to do helping those I love. I want to be a person who can look forward to living, instead of the constant fear of dying inside. I just want a place of calm and contentment, joy, love, and serenity. I just want Peace."

"Lord, I give my Life to you, your will Lord, not mine, be done."

"Thank you," I whispered as a new chill touches me. I had just asked God to help me find a way out and he did. The cold wind continued to blow against the T-shirts and shorts I had on; I was dressed for summer, as it had been the Labor Day weekend when I returned to jail this last time. I kept walking and shivering in the low forty-degree temperatures. I had no money in my pockets because the county takes any money they find on us and claims it for court costs. So, the few hundred dollars I had was now history;

it probably went in the pocket of the cop who was doing the booking, but that's just a guess.

Determined not to repeat any of my old life, I felt a real sense of loneliness as a tear rolled down my cheek, and a cold emptiness began running thru me. I was really close to having a complete emotional breakdown and almost jumped out of my skin when I heard a horn blow.

Kurt had stopped in the road and was trying to figure out why I was all the way out here instead of where he told me to stay. After all those years oblivious to a passing car, unless I was intentionally trying to get their attention, I mostly walked in a daze. I didn't really realize a car was there or that it was him. I was still trying to figure out what to do and where to go – back to Broadway, drugs, and that evil money or... and this was the million-dollar question.

> "What do I do now to change my life?"

After years of rehabs, including the one I had just finished I knew exactly what was required to have a new life in recovery. The question was how to make it work from the dark place I was in and desperately trying to leave behind. I was startled back to reality by Kurt's horn; I looked up at the car and saw Kurt watching me. He said later that he was wondering to himself whether this really was a good idea or not. He rolled down his window, and said, "Girl, why didn't you wait for me somewhere warm? Sorry I'm late, but it took forever for the girl to make this," and he held up a paper bag as the smell of food whooshes out the window, "I stopped to get you something to eat."

Truly stunned by Kurt's kindness. I just stared at him when another shiver shook my insides and more goosebumps formed on my cold skin. God had sent me one of His angels and at that moment I knew it. I will meet others along this path; good people just wanting to help me find my way. I had the strangest feeling as I looked at him from outside the car window; it was a feeling that almost consumed me. I have done this before in a bad way many times, as I reached out for that car door handle and it unnerved me just a bit. I quickly shook off the negative feeling as I pulled on the handle and opened the door of his car idling in the road.

This new friend, my angel at this moment was definitely a blessing. There are good people in the world, and it was time that I gave life a chance again. There will be much work ahead for me and I was ready to do it, whatever it took, even though I had absolutely no idea how hard my road actually would be. Trust was something I would have to focus on after the years of abuse I had suffered through, but I could not have been more grateful for Kurt's kindness and help right now.

Smiling at him as I opened the door to a new life, I felt safe with a man for only the second time in my life. Still amazed by the whole thing, I said, "Wow, thank you so much I am hungry for some real food this is great. You're so sweet." As I enjoyed the sandwich from Dunkin Donuts, I realized that Kurt had remembered they were my favorite. The night he last saw me we had gone to get food after he had picked me up out of the rain; it was also the same night he had given me his phone number again and said to call him anytime. As the radio played softly I ate my food and polished off the O.J., as Kurt tried to ask me a few questions as gently as he could. When I was finally finished with my food I was able to answer all of his questions.

"It feels nice in here," the car heater was running, and I had warmed quickly. Smiling, I said, "I didn't know who else to call, and you said to call you anytime. I'm sorry to have bothered you, but I want to try a better way at life, as you said, and make this work. I've been alone and in survival mode at its most savage of existence for so long. I'm ready for a change. I know this is asking a lot from you, but I just need a few hours to think and be somewhere safe."

Still dazed by his kindness, I hadn't really heard any of his questions. But, I was going to have to trust that I was going to be alright as long as I had faith in God, my Higher Power, and blessed by that Power daily!

In the rooms of AA or NA, they tell you to pray to a Higher Power and have faith that what you ask for will come true. They also tell you that working the steps laid out in the Big Book will help and they did, so I took what worked for me and applied it to my new life.

I, Tiffy Rose Baker, always knew God was with me even through my darkest times, and I continue to trust God will always be with me. My daily prayers of gratitude make this a feeling of completeness for me, a belonging that was absent all my life before I fully embraced this as my truth in life.

Finally, I look at Kurt, and ask, "I hope this is okay with your wife?" I asked mostly to gauge what problems might exist because honestly, most of my clientele were married men, and well, we had never really talked of his personal life before. I knew that everything about my old life would now have to disappear in order for me to change; I didn't want to depend on my previous work to take me from here to where I wanted to go.

First, he looked at me somewhat strange, and he just laughed, before he said, "Yes, I'm okay helping you for the night." I was relieved, but I wondered why he laughed. It was a relief to know that I would have tonight to come up with some kind of a plan, and I was so happy I did not have to go back to the living Hell down there on the Stroll.

It was ironic how once upon a time I had escaped life to live on the streets in order to get away from responsibility and order. Now, I was looking to run from addiction, back to responsibility and order. Funny, huh?

He had taken his time getting to his house, or maybe it just seemed that way to me. He found me some clothes to change into and said, "Why don't you go take a nice hot shower and relax? If you feel that you want to; it will be okay." I couldn't believe how sweet this guy is; was the thought running through my head as I stood in the middle of his living room. He said, "I'll put a blanket and pillow on the couch if you want to rest or watch TV. I'll be in the other room if you need anything. Make yourself at home, I trust you." He trusted me, wow, I could hardly believe what he said.

This was a man who was practically a stranger and when I heard that, it warmed my heart. And what's more the strangest thing happened, I did feel at home. As I found my way to the bathroom with the clothes and towel I whispered to myself, "Thank you, Lord."

Scrubbing off the jailhouse stench and the past years on the street, I must have stood in the shower for half an hour as the hot water warmed my soul, cleansing me both outside and in. I was in a safe place, a place where I might get the chance to set my recovery in motion, I thought.

As I was lying on his couch, and resting comfortably for the first time in well... I could not even remember. I knew I was eventually going to have to ask him how long I could stay, but the next morning after he made me some breakfast Kurt asked me; what I wanted and how he could help? Wow, how he could help, my mind was racing. He really seemed to want to help, and I was in awe of his kindness. I really did need someplace to stay and a few weeks to plan the work ahead, and then work, the plan I created. Trusting that I needed to take advantage of any help I could get, I said, "Right now, I just need time to think and a place to stay until I can get some things in order, and I am able to support myself the right way again." The silence was frightening, as I could almost hear the wheels spinning in his head, and I wondered if this was going to be my quick exit out the door. Although, it would prove to be just the opposite.

It was a new beginning, a second chance that had been given to me. To have the strength to stand on my own and be at peace inside, even with the wreckage of the past this was an ultimate gift from God. The weight of the horrible life that had been dragging behind me has become less and less each day, and maybe one day, I won't feel any of it any longer.

Kurt and I built a strong friendship, and I was truly grateful for all his help. The years we spent together were valuable to my recovery and his, as the PTSD he suffered from and all the violence as a combat veteran was an unnerving echo of his own past. To be free from this trap was going to take careful work and would be my top priority. The time I would have to process my new life was invaluable to my recovery. The planning I did and the steps I laid out to follow put into place the foundation of peace that I know today.

Freedom from my trap was *accomplished* by dedication and determination.

Learning to trust myself was learning that nothing I would face while rebuilding my life was as treacherous as the life I left behind in Addiction. The challenges will be many, but the results empowered me unlike any high I ever experienced. I had to remind myself of this often and in the end, no matter how many times I was frustrated with the slow pace, I stayed true to my new path.

Patience is paramountEverything happens in God's time, not mine, I had to reiterate often to myself.

Life in recovery is an amazing experience because it's almost as if you are a newborn. Your senses come alive, and your experiences are fresh and new. Recovery has given me a wonderful life, unlike anything I could have imagined. Because I trust in my Higher Power, I am able to keep going in a positive direction daily.

Time. Trust. Faith. Patience.

I remind myself of these things knowing recovery from addiction is not an overnight fix or a scheduled event. You have to fully engage in the process, or you can't get mad at the results.

Something softly reminds me on those occasions, usually at night, when the physical pain from my injuries over a lifetime are unbearable, or where those haunting dreams of using slither in and try to bother me, **why** do I pray. So I don't fail myself. "Oh God, please remove this pain and triggering thoughts from me.

Thank you for all you do in my life. Please, help me sleep." I hear myself say laying there in the quiet darkness.

As time passed and goals were fulfilled I was more comfortable with my new life. I became stronger and more confident in myself and continued my quest to one day own a home of my own. I was off to build my world and I knew it was going to take continued careful steps, that follow-through would be required to achieve the dreams and goals I had already set for myself.

I knew I wanted it, now was the time to figure out how and what were the steps to take in order to achieve it. I learned of a government grant program, sponsoring low-income housing assistance to home-buyers. "Well, heck, sign me up."

Here is the breakdown of what was required to qualify: a credit score of 720 or higher; one full year of employment with the same company to show stability; money in a savings account was a plus, but not required; $500 down and a checking account. I didn't qualify on my first attempt, but I stayed positive. At the time, my credit was improving, and I needed to be at the same job for at least one year before an application could be filled out again. I set out to complete these goals and continued to make my recovery my top priority on a daily basis.

Rose ... is what my friends now called me.

A fresh new perspective to a new life was needed, to travel from where I once lived, into the new world I wanted to attain.

Over the seven years that Kurt committed his life to helping me achieve safety in order to grow, learn and adjust to all the limitations my life would now hold because of my physical injuries. There are not enough words for the gratitude or trust I felt. A lesson that was probably the most critical for my growth forward, trusting that helping hand.

Our story and my ultimate ability to trust myself continues in FREE 'D a recovery plan, as it lays out the healing that takes place for myself, my family, Kurt, and eventually all those who shared in my recovery journey.

Freedom and Recovery

FREE'D ... from its grasp,
I escaped the Big Trap of Addiction and looked forward to my new life in Recovery.

Join me as I delve deeper in my personal journey and the work it took, the rebuilding and redemptive steps, I followed to have the life I do today, that you can follow too. The journey was not without its challenges, nor will yours be, but the outcome is truly a miracle of God and determination of a new soul blessed with a second chance. Yours can be too.

I will share in my next book additional knowledge and recovery steps from the professional resources, I was given on my journey.

Many Blessing to you all,
Rose

Expected release date January 2019

Hotline Information

Help Hotline Info
1. NA Worldwide Services Hotline (818) 773-9999
2. AA World Services Hotline (212) 870-3400
3. USA- National Domestic Abuse Hotline (800) 799-7233
4. USA- National Coalition for the Homeless Helpline (202) 462-4822
5. 24/7/365 Crisis National Hotline (800) 273-8255
6. SAMHSA- Substance Abuse and Mental Health Services Administration
USA- [National Hotline] (800) 662-4357

www.ingramcontent.com/pod-product-compliance
Lightning Source LLC
Chambersburg PA
CBHW071200070526
44584CB00019B/2866